Camping Arizona

Bruce Grubbs

FALCON®

HELENA, MONTANA

A FALCON GUIDE ®

Falcon® Publishing is continually expanding its list of recreational guidebooks. All books include detailed descriptions, accurate maps, and all information necessary for enjoyable trips. You can order extra copies of this book and get information and prices for other Falcon® books by writing Falcon, P.O. Box 1718, Helena, MT 59624, or by calling toll-free 1-800-582-2665. Also, please ask for a copy of our current catalog. Visit our website at www.FalconOutdoors.com or contact us by e-mail at falcon@falcon.com.

© 1999 Falcon® Publishing, Inc., Helena, Montana.
Printed in the United States of America.

1 2 3 4 5 6 7 8 9 0 MG 04 03 02 01 00 99

Falcon and FalconGuide are registered trademarks of Falcon® Publishing, Inc.

All black-and-white photos by the author unless otherwise noted.

Library of Congress Cataloging-in-Publication Data

Grubbs, Bruce (Bruce O.)
    Camping Arizona / by Bruce Grubbs.
        p.   cm. — (A Falcon guide)
    Includes index.
    ISBN 1-56044-712-5 (pbk.)
        1. Camp sites, facilities, etc.—Arizona Directories.
I. Title.   II. Series: Falcon guide.
GV191.42.A7G88   1999
647.94791'09'025—dc21   99-22910
                                                              ⏤ CIP

CAUTION
Outdoor recreational activities are by their very nature potentially hazardous. All participants in such activities must assume responsibility for their own actions and safety. The information contained in this guidebook cannot replace sound judgment and good decision-making skills, which help reduce exposure, nor does the scope of this book allow for the disclosure of all the potential hazards and risks involved in such activities.

Learn as much as possible about the outdoor recreational activities in which you participate, prepare for the unexpected, and be cautious. The reward will be a safer and more enjoyable experience.

 Text pages printed on recycled paper.

Contents

Acknowledgments

My parents deserve the most credit, for taking me camping and treating me to the delights of the outdoors at an early age. I also wish to thank my friends, who over the years have shared many camps with me. Warm thanks to Duart Martin for encouraging this project. Special thanks to Jean Rukkila for reading the manuscript; she not only found errors but also added personal comments on some of the campgrounds. I greatly appreciate all the agency personnel who took the time to answer my queries, and then reviewed my descriptions of their campgrounds for accuracy; you are too numerous to mention, but this book would not have been possible without you. Special thanks to Gail Shirley and Peggy O'Neill-McLeod, my editors, for their patience and understanding during this project. And finally, thanks to production editor, Brynlyn Lehmann, and the graphics and production people at Falcon Publishing for their work in turning a rough manuscript into another FalconGuide.

How to Use This Guide

If you're looking for a concise, easy-to-use guide to the public campgrounds in Arizona, this is your book. This FalconGuide is divided into seven major geographic divisions, each with its own unique characteristics—deserts, mountains, lakes, and so forth. Within the divisions, campgrounds are covered by areas. Each area has a map showing campground locations, a quick reference table showing campground facilities, and a description of each campground. There are photos of each area so that you can visualize the type of country you'll be camping in. You can use the geographic divisions map at the front of the book to choose the type of area appropriate to the season and your preferences. Use the map of that particular division to pick the area you'd like to camp in. Refer to the quick reference table and descriptions to get information on a specific campground, and compare it to others. Finally, use the campground map to locate the campground. Or, you can riffle through the book until you find a photo that catches your eye, and then look for campgrounds in that area.

This book covers Arizona public campgrounds with developed sites that are accessible by vehicle. Group campgrounds available by reservation only are not included, but if group camping in or near public campgrounds is available, it is mentioned in the campground description. Backcountry, hike-in campgrounds are not included; neither are informal campsites, campgrounds without developed sites, private campgrounds, nor RV parks found in the state. (For private campgrounds, I recommend *Woodall's Campground Directory for North America*, which is revised annually.)

If you encounter changes in campgrounds or errors in the book, I'd like to hear from you. Please contact me via Falcon Publishing, at the address in the front of the book.

ARIZONA GEOGRAPHIC DIVISIONS MAP

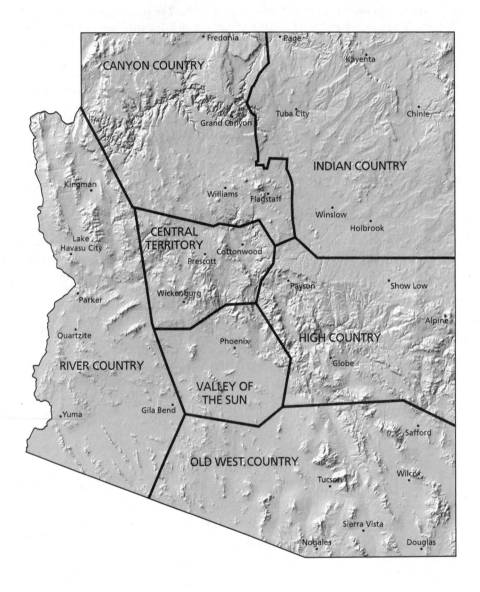

LEGEND

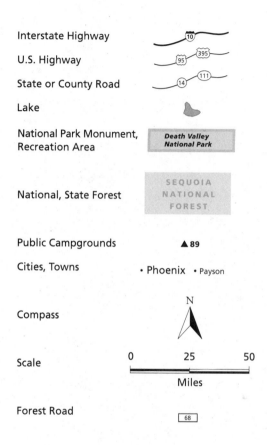

Interstate Highway

U.S. Highway

State or County Road

Lake

National Park Monument, Recreation Area

National, State Forest

Public Campgrounds   ▲ 89

Cities, Towns   • Phoenix   • Payson

Compass   N

Scale   0   25   50   Miles

Forest Road   68

Abbreviations

AZ	State highway
BLM	Bureau of Land Management
CR	County road
FR	Forest road (USFS)
I	Interstate highway
NPS	National Park Service
US	U.S. highway
USFS	U.S. Forest Service
FH	Forest Highway

Camping in Arizona

Arizona is a fascinating place in which to camp, because of the state's variety of topography and ecosystems. You'll find high, forested plateaus, alpine mountains, deep canyons, spacious deserts, as well as rivers, streams, and lakes.

Because of the large variations of elevation in the state, Arizona always has delightful weather somewhere, year-round. By picking your destination, you can enjoy perfect weather for your camping trip during any season.

During the summer, the low deserts in the central and southwest portions of the state are very hot. Temperatures often climb over the 110-degree F mark, and sometimes pass 120 degrees F in the lowest, hottest locations. Camping in these conditions is only enjoyable by a lake or a river where you can enjoy water sports. For that reason, most summer camping in the desert regions is done along the Colorado River and the reservoirs along the river. Other lakes in the central part of the state are also popular. Most campers head for the mountains of southeast, central, northern, and eastern Arizona during the summer. Here you can camp in the shade and majesty of the world's largest ponderosa pine forest. Sometime in July, the hot dry weather of early summer gives way to the Arizona monsoon. Seasonal moisture moves into the state from the southeast and commonly triggers afternoon thunderstorms. Mornings in the mountains are usually clear and cool during the monsoon. By late morning, cumulus clouds begin to fill the sky, and thunderstorms may develop by afternoon. The storms are usually brief, lasting an hour or so, but the rainfall may be intense and accompanied by lightning and even hail. After the rain stops, the mountain air is cool and sweet, and monsoon evenings are usually delightful.

During the autumn season, you can camp nearly anywhere in the state and enjoy good weather. The monsoon normally ends around mid-September as dry, cool air moves into the state. The mountains are still warm and pleasant during the day, though nights will be cold. As fall colors start to appear in the quaking aspen, Arizona sycamore, and other deciduous trees, mountain forests take on their most striking appearance of the year. In deserts, the hot temperature of summer moderates to merely warm, and the nights are cool.

By late November, the first winter storms drop snow in the mountains and rain in the desert, but seldom last more than a day or two. The dry periods between storms commonly last a week or more, and camping in the desert and moderate elevation areas (up to about 5,000 feet) is usually very pleasant. Though winter nights in the desert can verge on cold, the warm southern sun makes the days pleasant and enjoyable. Mountains and plateaus above 7,000 feet often have snow on the ground, and back roads are usually muddy or snowy and impassable. Nevertheless, a few mountain campgrounds stay open all year for those who want a snow camping experience.

Snowstorms are possible in the mountains as late as May, but usually the weather dries out in April. By mid-May most of the high country is free of snow and back roads are dry and passable. After wet winters, desert country is a riot of wildflowers, starting as early as February in lower desert areas, and continuing into April in higher deserts and grasslands. It's a show you don't want to miss. In spring, desert temperatures are still moderate and mountains have warmed up, so you can camp nearly anywhere in the state.

Public campgrounds. Public campgrounds in Arizona are run by several government agencies. Federal agencies include the National Park Service (NPS), the USDA Forest Service, and the Bureau of Land Management (BLM). The State of Arizona maintains a number of campgrounds through the state park system. In addition, several counties and cities operate public campgrounds.

The BLM has designated several Long Term Visitor Areas (LTVA) in Arizona. These are special areas where camping is allowed for longer than the usual 14-day limit. LTVAs do not generally have developed facilities.

Group camping areas. Some campgrounds have special group areas; other campgrounds are set aside for the use of groups only. These areas usually require advance reservation. Call the managing agency well in advance to ensure getting your preferred dates.

Reservations. Some campgrounds accept reservations, while others are first-come, first-served. Reservations can be made for many campgrounds by calling Park Net at 877-444-6777. Otherwise, contact the managing agency at the number listed in the campground description. National Park Service campground reservations are also available on the Internet at http://reservations.nps.gov.

Dispersed camping. Dispersed camping, which is camping away from developed campground facilities, is permitted on some federal lands, primarily those administered by the Forest Service and the BLM. Certain areas may be closed to dispersed camping; these are usually designated recreation areas. National parks and monuments run by the National Park Service and Arizona state parks do not usually allow dispersed camping.

There are large areas of the state, especially in the western deserts, where there are no developed campgrounds, so going out on your own is the only way to enjoy camping in these beautiful areas. The experience can be very rewarding and it certainly gets you away from crowds. Dispersed campers have special responsibilities. You'll have to be completely self-contained. It may be many miles to the nearest point of resupply. Since there is no trash disposal or site maintenance other than what you provide, you must minimize your impact. Use the following guidelines to ensure that the next camper will find your campsite as good as or better than you found it.

- Cook on a camp stove—it's cleaner and more convenient than a campfire.

- Keep your campfire small.

- Use existing fire rings rather than building new ones.

- Pick up dead wood from the ground. Don't saw or chop on standing dead trees. Many species of wildlife depend on dead trees for homes.

- Do not burn trash. Many plastics give off toxic fumes when burned. Aluminum does not burn—it melts into silvery blobs that remain forever. Many food packages are lined with aluminum.

- Do not bury trash. Animals will smell it and dig it up soon after you leave.

- Pick a tent site with natural drainage—on a slight slope or slightly domed patch of ground—so that you do not have to dig ditches.

- Do not drive or camp on meadows. The vegetation is fragile and scars last many years.

- Carry and use a portable toilet, unless you're in a self-contained RV or trailer.

- If you have to answer the call of nature where there are no facilities, go well away from your campsite. Pick a spot at least 300 feet from open water and away from dry washes. Avoid dry, sandy areas if possible. Dig a small "cat hole" about 6 inches deep. Double-bag and carry out used toilet paper (baking soda helps control odor). When finished, cover the hole and restore the surface cover.

Camping with kids. Why camp with your kids? There are a lot of good reasons. First of all, kids like to camp. I know I did when I was a kid. What may be a pretty ordinary campground to you is a world full of adventure to a child. If you can choose a campground with special appeal to your kids, so much the better. A kid who is interested in dinosaurs will be fascinated by fossil dinosaur tracks or a dinosaur quarry. Don't overlook kid attractions in nearby towns, either. A trip to a hands-on science or natural history museum will make a camping trip memorable for kids, even though the trip takes you a few miles from your campsite.

Camping gets your kids into nature. If they grow up camping, they will grow up being comfortable in the outdoors. They might even take up other outdoor sports on their own as they get older. And what is good for the kids is good for the whole family. Today's pace of life and its demands on us make it hard for families to spend time together. Camping naturally brings families together. Finally, camping is a cheap way for the family to vacation together. Even the most expensive campground is low-cost, compared to lodges and motels. You will save even more money cooking your own camp meals. And it doesn't hurt to be away from malls and other shopping temptations, if your kids are teenagers.

Planning a camping trip with kids is a little different from planning a trip for adults. Remember that most kids naturally like camping, so you have an advantage right from the beginning. Your challenge is to keep it interesting. Start by easing into camping. Take the kids on a few weekend outings before committing to a month-long camping vacation. Find campgrounds near home to avoid long drives. Look for campgrounds that will be especially interesting to your kids, as mentioned above. Make the trip comfortable for the kids and the adults. Choose a campground where the weather will be pleasant. Also avoid camping where there are a lot of insects such as mosquitoes. Generally, bugs are only a problem in the mountains the first couple of weeks after snow melt. Remember your children's limited attention spans. Lounging around all day in a camp chair with a good book may be your idea of paradise, but your kids will get bored in about a minute. Include physical activities such as games or nature explorations. Let your kids help with camp chores. Because there are hazards in the outdoors that kids have to learn to recognize, you will need to set rules that are different from those used at home.

What age is old enough to camp? That depends on you. Some parents take infants and others wait until the kids are in school. Younger kids are more work for you, but you will make a greater impression on them. In Scandinavia, kids are taken out on sleds before they can walk by their cross-country skiing parents. They learn to ski and walk almost at the same time. No wonder the Scandinavian countries produce so many winter sports Olympians!

Camping with your kids takes more effort on your part, but your reward is the wonder of watching your kids discover nature and the outdoors.

Safety tips. While camping in Arizona is a very safe activity, a few precautions will ensure that your camping experience is an enjoyable one.

Fire hazard. During certain seasons, the forest and range fire hazard can be very high. Fire danger is highest during late spring and early summer (May, June, and July) and during early fall (October and November). When fire danger reaches extreme levels, wildfires start easily and spread explosively. Land managers may close certain areas to all public access during these periods. **Don't be tempted to violate such fire closures.** Not only are you literally risking your life if a fire should start nearby, you will very likely be cited and fined if caught in a closed area. Luckily, most fire seasons do not reach such extreme levels. On the other hand, campfires are often restricted during late June and early July. Sometimes campfires are prohibited for dispersed campers but still allowed in official campgrounds. Occasionally campfires are prohibited everywhere. **Please observe all campfire restrictions** for your own safety and to preserve the beauty of the forests and rangelands.

Smoking may also be prohibited on public lands during high fire danger. In certain extreme fire danger situations, smoking **while traveling on foot or horseback may be prohibited in national forests.** During these particular situations, Forest Service regulations require that you stop and clear a three-foot diameter area to bare soil before smoking, and that you extinguish all smoking materials before moving on. The Forest Service encourages you to do so all year, because Arizona forests and grasslands can be dry any time of year. In addition, Arizona state law makes it illegal to throw burning materials, including cigarettes, from a moving vehicle. There are fire scars along most highways in Arizona that graphically show why these rules are necessary.

Weather. Hot weather is a serious hazard during the summer months in the desert. Even in the mountains, the hot summer sun and dry air can lead to heat-related injuries such as heat exhaustion and sunstroke. Water is precious and scarce in the desert and even the mountains are not as well watered as you might expect. Because of this, many campgrounds do not have water supplies. (The availability of water is listed in the campground tables.) In the off-season, campground water supplies may be turned off to prevent freezing or because of a lack of funds to maintain them. If you plan to stay in a campground without a water supply, make sure you carry enough water in your vehicle to last your stay. During the hot half of the year (April through September), the wise Arizona traveler carries at least a couple of gallons of water in his or her vehicle in case of breakdown or becoming stranded. This is especially important for travel off paved highways. During hot weather in the desert, your survival time without water is measured in hours.

Late summer brings thunderstorms to the state. The accompanying lightning is dangerous, and you should take refuge in a safe place, such as your vehicle, during thunderstorms. If caught in the open, avoid lone trees and high ground. Find the lowest nearby area, then squat on the ground with your feet together until the lightning passes. The heavy rain from thunderstorms can cause normally dry washes to suddenly flood, often miles from the storm. Never camp or park your vehicle in dry washes.

Winter weather is a hazard in the Arizona mountains from November through mid-April. A major winter storm can quickly cause highways to become snow-packed and back roads to become impassable. Expect delays even on major highways due to snow plowing and accidents. If you do travel and camp in the mountains during the winter season, be prepared with extra clothing, blankets or sleeping bags, extra food and water, and tire chains or a four-wheel-drive vehicle. Keep a close eye on the weather forecast. A small weather radio that picks up broadcasts directly from the National Weather Service is a good investment.

Animals and plants

Many Arizona campgrounds provide special opportunities for viewing wildlife. These opportunities are mentioned in the campground description. Enjoy the wildlife, but please remember that you are a visitor in the outdoors when you are camping. What is a temporary outdoor home for you is the only home for wild animals and plants. Treat all wildlife with respect and caution. Most hazardous encounters with wild animals are a direct result of an irresponsible person.

Never approach or attempt to handle any wild animal. All animals will defend themselves if they feel threatened or cornered. Even rabbits will bite to protect their young. By approaching or harassing wildlife, you are placing great stress on the animal and endangering yourself. Never feed any wild animal, no matter how cute it seems, and do not allow children to feed animals. Human food is not good for them. Animals that become used to handouts lose their natural fear of humans and become camp robbers, endangering both you and your equipment.

Mountain lions. In Arizona, mountain lions are rare and elusive creatures in the remote country where they still survive. You will be lucky to see tracks, let alone the animal. The only cases of attack have been where the human aroused the lion's predatory instincts by appearing to be prey. Running and mountain biking in lion country seems to present a slight chance of evoking the same response that a running deer does. Also, children on their own may attract the attention of a mountain lion. If you do encounter a mountain lion, avoid prey-like reactions. Make yourself appear as big and threatening as possible, and make unnatural sounds by rattling metal pots or the like. Don't turn your back on the animal, and don't run. Mountain lion encounters usually result in just a fleeting glimpse of this magnificent animal.

Wolves and coyotes. The native Mexican gray wolf has been reintroduced in the mountains of eastern Arizona. They are not a hazard to humans. Neither are coyotes. The thrilling nocturnal howl of coyotes is as much a part of the Arizona backcountry as the clear, starry nights. We can only hope that the wolves take hold in their former ranges and that we will be lucky enough to hear their song as well.

Domestic cattle. Public land, especially national forest, BLM, and state land, is often used for grazing, so you are likely to encounter cattle. Generally, cattle are used to humans, and either avoid them or move away. It is possible that a bull could be dangerous, so it's a good idea to give cattle a reasonable margin. Grazing is generally not allowed in national parks and monuments.

Snakes and other reptiles. Arizona rattlesnakes are fascinating animals, well-adapted for life in the harsh environment. Rattlesnakes do not attack people unless they feel threatened. They may accidentally crawl in your direction if they are not aware of your presence. Rattlesnakes are more sensitive to ground vibrations than to sound, and ordinarily move quietly away from an approaching large animal, such as a hiker. If surprised, they usually coil into a defensive posture and back slowly away. The snake creates its unmistakable buzzing rattle by shaking its tail so fast it blurs. When you hear the rattle, stop immediately and spot the snake before moving carefully away. Never handle or tease any snake. Bites usually occur on the feet or hands; never step or place your hands in places you cannot see. The vast majority of rattlesnake bites are suffered by collectors. It is very rare for a camper to be bitten. Rattlesnake bites can be distinguished from nonpoisonous snake bites by the two puncture wounds left by the venomous fangs, in addition to the regular tooth marks.

The Sonoran coral snake is found only in the deserts of southern Arizona and northwestern Mexico. While extremely poisonous, it is reclusive, very small, and would have difficulty biting a human. All other snakes in Arizona are nonpoisonous, though they may bite if handled.

Snakes prefer surfaces at about 80 degrees F. During hot weather they prefer the shade of bushes or rock overhangs, and in cool weather will be found sunning themselves on open ground. During cold weather they are inactive. Any time lizards are active, rattlesnakes probably are active as well. Use a flashlight when moving around camp at dark, at least in the warmer months when snakes are active mainly at night. Never walk around camp barefoot or in sandals during that time of year.

Never kill rattlesnakes. They are a vital part of the desert ecology and should be treated with respect, and not feared unnecessarily. Do not handle a dead rattlesnake; they can strike by reflex for some time after apparent death.

A large lizard, the Gila monster, possesses a venom similar to that of rattlesnakes, but instead of striking, it clamps onto its victim and grinds the venom into the wound with its molars. A rare and elusive reptile about a foot long and protected by state law, the Gila monster is likely to bite only if handled or molested. Do not let its torpid appearance fool you—it can move very fast.

If someone in your party is bitten by a poisonous snake or a Gila monster, keep the victim calm and transport him or her to a hospital as soon as possible.

Insects. Poisonous insects and spiders are actually a greater hazard in Arizona than rattlesnakes. The small, straw-colored desert scorpion likes to lurk under rocks and logs, and its sting can be life-threatening to children. Black widow spiders, identifiable by the red hourglass-shaped mark on the underside, can inflict a dangerous bite. The brown spider (sometimes called the brown recluse) is pale tan or yellow and often has a violin-shaped mark on its head. It inflicts a bite that can cause extensive tissue damage but is not generally life-threatening. These bites seem minor at first but may become very painful after several hours.

There is no specific field treatment; young children should be transported to a hospital as soon as possible.

The larger, more common scorpions have a painful sting, but are not as dangerous as the small scorpions. The ferocious-looking centipede can produce a painful bite, and can also irritate skin with its sharp, clawed feet, but it is not life-threatening.

Scorpions, spiders, and centipedes can be almost completely avoided by taking a few simple precautions. Avoid placing your hands and feet where you cannot see them. Kick over rocks or logs before moving them with your hands. Don't unpack your sleeping bag before you need it in the evening, and always shake out clothing and footwear in the morning before dressing.

Kissing bugs, also known as cone-nose bugs or assassin bugs, are obnoxious insects about $1/2$ to 1 inch long and brown or black in color. They live in rodent nests and feed on mammal blood at night, leaving a large, itchy welt on the victim. They are only a problem if you sleep under the stars without a tent or other shelter.

Ticks occur rarely in Arizona. If ticks are discovered, though, do a careful full-body search every day. It's important to remove imbedded ticks before they have a chance to transmit disease, which takes a day or more to take hold.

Other insects, such as bees, velvet ants, wasps, and the like, give painful but nonthreatening stings. The exception is for people who have a known allergic reaction to specific insect stings. Such people should carry insect sting kits prescribed by their doctors, since reactions can develop rapidly and become life-threatening.

A new hazard has recently appeared in Arizona, the Africanized honey bee. These bees were accidentally introduced into Brazil in the 1960s, and have since spread north to Texas and Arizona. They are expected to continue spreading across the warmer deserts. Because of their tropical origins, Africanized bees are sensitive to cold and are not likely to become numerous in higher desert mountains and plateaus, but it is possible that a camper could encounter Africanized bees in lower desert areas. Popularly known as killer bees, they have been responsible for about 1,000 human deaths in the Western hemisphere, but only a few in the United States. In comparison, the common European honey bees cause about 100 deaths per year in the United States. Although the Africanized bee's venom is no more toxic than the common European honey bee's, they are more aggressive in defending their hives and will sometimes swarm on or chase an intruder. The hazard to a person who is allergic to bee stings is obvious. Every documented fatal case in the Western hemisphere has involved an allergic individual, or someone who was infirm or otherwise unable to escape. I have yet to hear of any serious encounter between Africanized bees and campers.

Avoid all beehives. This includes cultivated bees, which may be a mixture of both types. Cultivated beehives are stacks of white boxes, always found near roads. Wild bees build hives in rock crevices and in holes in trees. Always avoid swarming bees. If attacked, protect your eyes and run away. If shelter such as a tent, vehicle, or building is available, use it. Africanized bees apparently don't pursue more than half a mile.

There are many scary-looking desert insects that, in reality, are not dangerous—millipedes, whip scorpions, Jerusalem crickets, sun spiders, and tarantulas, for example. They look ferocious but are not a threat to humans.

Plants. Plant hazards are easily avoided. Never eat any plant. Some areas have stinging nettles, which as the name implies do not feel good on the skin. Check carefully before sitting or lying on the ground in nettle areas. In some areas, poison ivy grows seasonally along streams and moist drainages. The oil found on the leaves and stems causes a severe skin reaction in many people. Poison ivy is easily recognized by its shiny, green leaves, which grow in groups of three.

Slow-growing desert plants have developed an interesting array of defenses to protect themselves and their precious moisture from animals, birds, and insects that would like to dine on them. Spines and thorns are some of the obvious features of cacti and cacti-like plants. Most spines are needlelike, and an encounter results in a simple puncture. Teddy bear cholla (sometimes called jumping cholla) found in the Sonoran desert of central and southwestern Arizona looks cute and cuddly. It's not. Each branch is covered with thousands of slender spines, each of which has invisible barbs. If a burr sticks to your skin or clothing, remove it with a pocket comb or a pair of sticks. Then, use a good pair of tweezers to pick out the remaining spines. If the spines become deeply imbedded, seek medical attention.

Use care around plants with large, spine-tipped leaves, such as the agaves and yuccas. The spines can cause deep puncture wounds if you accidentally stumble into them, or grab one as a handhold. The edges of the stiff leaves often have hooked thorns that can cause nasty scratches or deeper wounds. Some small cacti, such as the aptly named pincushion cactus, are small, straw colored, and tend to hide in grass. They are a particular hazard when scrambling up rocky areas.

Catclaw is a bush that sometimes grows in dense thickets. The sharp, curved thorns catch on clothing and skin and have to be carefully peeled off. Long-sleeved shirts and pants help, but it is best to avoid thickets altogether.

Mineshafts

Arizona has always been attractive to miners and prospectors because of the expanses of bare, often mineralized rock. As a result, abandoned mine shafts and prospect holes are common in some areas. While land managers and mining authorities are making an attempt to secure dangerous sites, the sheer vastness of the problem leaves a lot of hazards. **Never enter any mine shaft.** Besides the obvious hazard of collapse, old mines often contain poisonous or radioactive gases, as well as unstable explosives and dangerous equipment. Report any explosives or other unusual hazards to the land management agency after your trip. The presence of an old road, even if closed and now part of designated wilderness, may be a sign that there are old mines in the area.

In heavy brush, or at night, be especially alert for old mine shafts. In areas that have attracted a lot of prospecting, miners often dig numerous small pits.

Even though these pits are usually only a few feet deep, coming upon one unaware can result in ankle or leg injuries or worse. In mined areas, stay away from the edges of vertical shafts, even if covered. The edges of shafts often continue to crumble for years after abandonment. Also avoid depressions in the ground—these may mark shafts or pits that have been covered with wood or metal that is rotting or rusting away.

Camping etiquette

Picking a campsite. Try to arrive at your chosen campground early so you'll have plenty of time to find a good site. When you enter the campground, check the bulletin board or entrance station for any special regulations. Many national forest campgrounds are self-serve. In this case, drive around the campground until you find a site you like. Leave someone, or a piece of gear such as a cooler, at the campsite so that others will know that it is occupied while you go back to the entrance and pay the fee.

Sometimes you will arrive late because of circumstances you cannot avoid. In this case, avoid excessive driving around the campground while looking for a site, and dim your headlights. Your fellow campers will appreciate it.

Leave No Trace. Always use trash receptacles. Some campgrounds do not have trash removal services. In this case, you must carry out all your trash. **Never** bury food scraps, packaging, or any sort of trash. Animals will dig up anything with a food odor. **Never** burn trash in a campfire. Many packaging materials contain thin layers of aluminum, which does not burn in even the hottest campfire. Like plastic, it fuses into small blobs. Popular camping areas are scarred with numerous old fire pits that glitter with bits of aluminum and plastic. Also, some plastics give off highly toxic fumes when burned.

Carry out trash left by careless or thoughtless people, especially when camping away from developed campgrounds. For this, a few extra garbage bags and a pair of gloves are handy. Then you can bask in the glow of self-righteous pleasure!

Maximum number of people and vehicles per campsite. Many campgrounds impose limits on the number of people that may occupy a campsite. Likewise, the number of vehicles may be limited. Always observe these limits out of respect for your fellow campers.

Campfire restrictions. As mentioned earlier, campfire restrictions may be in effect during periods of high fire danger. Although fire restrictions usually apply only to campfires outside of developed campgrounds, in some cases campfires may be prohibited in designated campsites as well. Even if restrictions are not in place, never build a fire on a windy day, or any other time you perceive the fire danger to be high.

Stay limits. Nearly all campgrounds have posted stay limits, usually from 7 to 14 days. A few very popular sites have shorter stay limits, while designated long term camping areas may have stay limits of several months. Please observe the stay limits so that other campers can have their turn.

Quiet hours. Most campgrounds have posted quiet hours, which are usually between 10 P.M. and 6 A.M. During quiet hours try to avoid disturbing other campers; do not run generators, play radios or stereos, or make other loud noises.

Checkout time. Always observe the posted checkout time. If you have to stay later, check with the campground host or ranger to see if you need to pay an additional night's fee.

Picnicking in campgrounds. Never use campsites in campgrounds for picnicking. Some campgrounds have designated day-use areas; otherwise, use a picnic area for day use.

Respect other people. At all times, respect other people and treat them as you would like to be treated. During the busy season, certain campgrounds can become crowded. Respect other campers' desire for privacy. Think about your neighbors before you light that lantern, or shine that flashlight around.

Share space. All campgrounds have shared facilities, which may include restrooms, water taps, trash bins, sanitary disposal stations, and other facilities. Patiently wait your turn when other campers are ahead of you. Remember, part of the idea of camping is to leave the frantic pace of the city behind and exchange it for a more relaxed lifestyle!

Emergency phone numbers

The statewide emergency services number is 911. Use 911 only in an emergency. If you have a non-emergency call, use the administrative phone number for the agency you want. Some general numbers are in the text; the phone number of the managing agency of each campground is listed in the information block for that campground.

For the Arizona State Patrol, county sheriffs, road conditions, and National Weather Service, refer to your local phone book for the phone numbers in each area.

Organization of the book

The campgrounds in the book are divided into sections for each of the seven major geographic divisions of the state, developed by the Arizona Office of Tourism. Each division has a map showing the general area and a general description of the division. Most of the divisions are further divided into regions based on a city or town within the region. Each region has a map showing the locations of all its campgrounds. There is also a description of the region, its recreational opportunities, and the nature of camping in that part of the state. There is also a list of contact addresses and phone numbers for getting additional information.

Next, there is a campground chart that summarizes the facilities at each campground in an easy-to-read format. Items listed include the campground number and name; its elevation; season of use; availability of RV and trailer sites; the total number of sites; the availability of drinking water, fishing, RV dumps, hiking trails, boating, and boat launches; handicap accessibility; fees, if any; and the stay limit. Toilet facilities are available at all campgrounds, and so are tent camping sites.

Campground numbers are keyed to the regional map and to the detailed campground descriptions. Campground listings start at the northwest corner of each map, more or less, then proceed east and south. There are a few exceptions to this order, mainly when terrain and campground access make it reasonable to change the order slightly. Official agency campground names are used, but some maps and publications may show different or incorrect names. Campground elevations are shown in feet, and they help you determine the climate and best season for camping. Campgrounds below 4,000 feet are generally hot in summer, but pleasant in winter. Above 7,000 feet, they are usually snowbound in winter, and cool in summer. The "season" is the official agency season that the campground is open. Not all facilities may be available during the open season. If the RV/trailer column is blank, then only tent camping is available. The sites column lists the total number of sites, which may be divided between tent and RV/trailer sites. **Drinking water is not available in all campgrounds;** if it is, the drinking water column is checked. The water system may be turned off in cold weather or during the off-season, even though the campground is open. If either lake or stream fishing is available nearby, the fishing column is checked. Of course, the type and quality of fishing varies with the season and other conditions; check with the Arizona Department of Game and Fish local office for more information.

If a sanitary disposal station is available at the campground, the RV dump column is checked. In some cases a separate fee may be charged for this service. A check in the hiking trails column means that nature and/or hiking trails are available nearby. Nature trails are interpretive trails with signs or brochures that explain local nature features. Such trails are great for getting to know the local flora and fauna. Hiking trails are generally longer trails that can be used for day hikes and backpack trips. The boating column indicates whether boating is available nearby. This may be either river or lake boating; the campground description will have detailed information. The boat launch column indicates whether or not a public boat ramp and launching facility are available. Handicap access, if checked, means that at least one campsite is wheelchair-accessible.

A check in the fee column means that a fee is charged for each night's stay. The specific campground fee is not shown, as fees are subject to change. Campground fees generally vary with the amount and quality of the facilities provided, with more developed campgrounds charging more. Even different sites within the same campground may have different fees. Some campgrounds have very basic facilities and charge no fee. Finally, the stay limit in days is shown.

Campground descriptions. Campground descriptions follow the campground services chart and are listed in the same order as the chart. An at-a-glance section gives several items of information about the campground. **Location** gives the campground's location in relation to the nearest town and appropriate natural features. **Sites** gives the number of tent and RV sites, the maximum RV or trailer length, and the number and type of hookups. If no maximum length is listed, the campground has no length restrictions. **Road conditions** describes whether the access roads are paved, all-weather dirt, dirt, or a combination. Paved and all-weather roads are normally passable in all weather, but some roads may be closed for the winter season. Dirt roads vary greatly in their condition and degree of maintenance, and are likely to become impassable in wet weather. Most dirt roads to campgrounds in this book are passable to ordinary vehicles in dry weather, if you drive with care. Exceptions are mentioned in the text. **Management** gives the name of the agency or unit that manages the campground, along with a phone number for obtaining current information. Many public campgrounds are now managed by private companies under contract; in some cases the contact number is for the private company. **Finding the campground** gives directions to the campground from a nearby town. Usually this is the same town that the section is based upon.

Description gives information such as nearby attractions, vegetation at the campground, the type of hiking trails, angling information, the availability of group camping, and showers. Finally, the nearest services are described. "Limited services" means that the described town or location does not have all the services you would expect from a city, such as repair garages and large supermarkets. You can expect to find small gas stations with limited hours, and small convenience markets in such places. The term "full services" means that repair shops, supermarkets, and other city amenities are available in this city.

Canyon Country

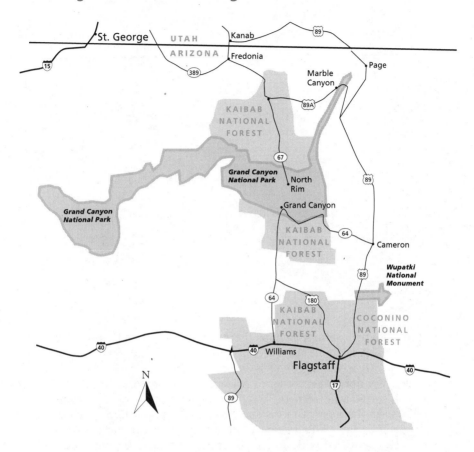

Arizona's Canyon Country includes the southwestern section of the Colorado Plateau, a vast land of deep canyons and high plateaus. It includes the north and south rims of Grand Canyon, the volcanic mountain country around Flagstaff and Williams, and the canyon-carved edge of the western Mogollon Rim. Grand Canyon's mile-deep, 300-mile long barrier isolates the plateau to the north from the rest of Arizona. On the east, at the upper end of the canyons, U.S. Highway 89A crosses the Colorado River near the historic site of Lees Ferry. The next crossing of the river and the canyons is 300 miles downstream at Hoover Dam on U.S. Highway 93.

NORTH RIM

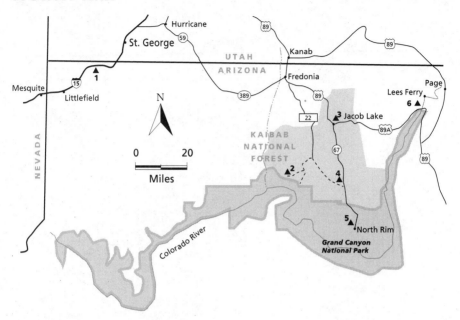

North Rim country is also known as the Arizona Strip, because of its isolation from the rest of Arizona. It often seems more a part of Utah than Arizona. The BLM's Virgin River Campground is located on Interstate 15 where it slices through the very northwest corner of Arizona on its way from Nevada to Utah. Get just a mile or so away from the busy freeway, and you're in the Arizona of 50 or 100 years ago. Because of its distance from major population centers, North Rim country is an uncrowded land. A star attraction for the camper is the high Kaibab Plateau, covered with an alpine forest of ponderosa pine, Douglas-fir, and quaking aspen. Kaibab is an old Paiute Indian word meaning "mountain lying down," and that's a perfect description of this vast plateau.

For more information:

Fredonia Chamber of Commerce

P.O. Box 547

100 N. Main

Fredonia, AZ 86022

(520) 643-7241

Fax (520) 643-7685

NORTH RIM

		Elevation	Season	RV/Trailer	Sites	Drinking Water	Fishing	RV dump	Hiking trails	Boating	Boat launch	Handicap access	Fee ($)	Stay limit (days)
1	Virgin River	1,900	All year	•	115	•			•				•	14
2	Indian Hollow	8,500	May-Nov	•	3				•					14
3	Jacob Lake	7,900	May-Nov	•	52	•			•			•	•	14
4	Demotte Park	9,000	May-Nov	•	22	•							•	14
5	North Rim	8,200	May-Oct	•	83	•			•				•	7
6	Lees Ferry	3,170	All year	•	54	•	•	•	•	•	•		•	14

1 Virgin River

Location: About 16 miles northeast of Littlefield, in the Virgin River Canyon.
Sites: 115 tent and RV. No hookups.
Road conditions: Paved.
Management: Bureau of Land Management, 435-688-3200.
Finding the campground: From Littlefield, Arizona, go 16 miles north on Interstate 15 and take the Cedar Pockets exit.

Description: Located in the spectacular Virgin River Gorge between the Beaver Dam Mountains and the Virgin Mountains, this campground's canyon setting seems especially wild if approached across the Mohave Desert from the south. The freeway forms a narrow corridor through the Beaver Dam and Paiute Wildernesses, so this campground is a good base for hiking and exploring. There are limited services in Littlefield and full services in St. George, Utah.

2 Indian Hollow

Location: Grand Canyon North Rim.
Sites: 3 tent and RV up to 32 feet. No hookups.
Road conditions: Paved, dirt.
Management: Kaibab National Forest, 520-643-7395.
Finding the campground: From Fredonia, drive about 1 mile east on U.S. Highway 89A, then turn right on Forest Road 22. After about 30 miles, turn right on Forest Road 425. Go 8 miles, then turn right on Forest Road 232 and continue 5 miles to its end.

Description: This tiny campground is primarily trailhead camping for the Thunder River Trail into Grand Canyon. It also makes a good base for exploring the western Kaibab Plateau and the scenic forest roads and trails. The nearest limited services are in Jacob Lake; full services are in Fredonia and Kanab.

A winter snowfall makes the rock formations of the Grand Canyon stand out in interesting relief.

3 Jacob Lake

Location: Jacob Lake on the Kaibab Plateau.
Sites: 52 tent and RV up to 32 feet. No hookups.
Road conditions: Paved.
Management: Kaibab National Forest, 520-643-7395.
Finding the campground: The campground is located at the tiny hamlet of Jacob Lake, at the junction of U.S. Highway 89A and Arizona Highway 67.

Description: Jacob Lake is the gateway to Grand Canyon National Park's North Rim, and the campground makes a fine base for daylong excursions into the park and the surrounding high plateau country. Naturalist programs are offered. There is a group campground, available by reservation only. Jacob Lake Inn, across the highway, has a restaurant, lodging, a service station, and limited supplies. The Forest Service Visitor Center, south of the Inn, can supply maps and information on the Kaibab National Forest. The nearest full services are in Fredonia and Kanab.

4 Demotte Park

Location: About 25 miles south of Jacob Lake, on the Kaibab Plateau.
Sites: 53 tent and RV up to 22 feet. No hookups.
Road conditions: Paved, dirt.
Management: Kaibab National Forest, 520-643-7395.

Finding the campground: From Jacob Lake on U.S. Highway 89A, go 25 miles south on Arizona Highway 67. Turn right just after passing Kaibab Lodge.

Description: The campground is set in the forest on the edge of Demotte Park, the largest of several beautiful alpine meadows on the Kaibab Plateau. Naturalist programs are available. Kaibab Lodge has lodging and a restaurant, and North Rim Country Store across the highway has limited supplies, and a service station. The nearest full services are in Fredonia and Kanab.

5 North Rim

Location: North Rim Grand Canyon.
Sites: 83 tent and RV sites. No hookups.
Road conditions: Paved.
Management: Grand Canyon National Park, 520-638-7808, 800-365-CAMP.
Finding the campground: From Jacob Lake on U.S. Highway 89A, go 43 miles south on Arizona Highway 67 to North Rim Village in Grand Canyon National Park.

Description: Although frequently full during the summer, this campground's location is hard to beat as a base for enjoying and exploring the North Rim of Grand Canyon. Lodging, restaurants, limited supplies, and a service station are nearby. The nearest full services are in Fredonia and Kanab.

6 Lees Ferry

Location: Marble Canyon
Sites: 54 tent and RV sites. No hookups.
Road conditions: Paved.
Management: Glen Canyon National Recreation Area, 520-608-6404.
Finding the campground: From Page, drive 25 miles south on U.S. Highway 89, then turn right on U.S. Highway 89A. Go 14 miles north to Marble Canyon, then turn right on Lees Ferry Road and continue 5 miles to the campground.

Description: Historic Lees Ferry was a major crossing point on the Colorado River until the ferry was replaced by Navajo Bridge in the 1920s. Hoover Dam, 300 miles downstream, is the next auto crossing on the Colorado River. Today, Lees Ferry is famous for its trout fishery, created by the cold water issuing from the depths of Lake Powell, behind Glen Canyon Dam. Lees Ferry is also the launch point for Grand Canyon raft trips. The setting is dramatic, under the towering, sandstone Vermilion and Echo Cliffs. Limited services, including gas, groceries, lodging, a restaurant, fishing guides, and a laundromat, are available at Marble Canyon; the nearest full services are in Page.

SOUTH RIM

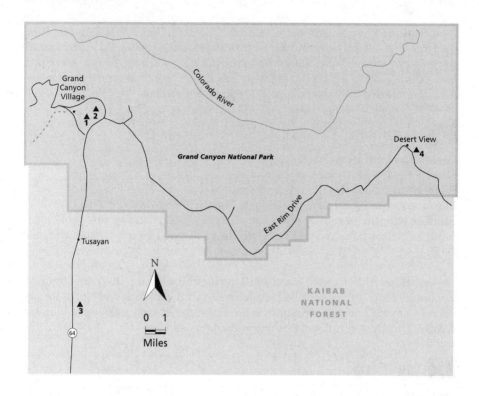

Grand Canyon's South Rim is by far the more accessible and popular of the two rims, and campground spaces are hard to come by during the summer. A good alternative is to stay in one of the campgrounds near Williams or Flagstaff and plan on a day trip to the South Rim. Off season, the South Rim is less crowded, and it is possible to stay in Mather Campground, leave your vehicle parked, and explore the canyon's rim by shuttle bus and foot.

For more information:
Grand Canyon Chamber of Commerce
P.O. Box 3007
Grand Canyon, AZ 86023
(520) 638-2901

SOUTH RIM

		Elevation	Season	RV/Trailer	Sites	Drinking Water	Fishing	RV dump	Hiking trails	Boating	Boat launch	Handicap access	Fee ($)	Stay limit (days)
1	Mather	7,100	All year	•	315	•			•				•	7
2	Trailer Village	7,100	All year	•	78	•		•	•				•	
3	Ten-X	6,600	May-Oct	•	70	•			•			•	•	14
4	Desert View	7,400	May-Oct	•	50	•			•				•	7

1 Mather

Location: Grand Canyon Village.
Sites: 315 tent and RV. No hookups.
Road conditions: Paved.
Management: Grand Canyon National Park, 520-638-7808, 800-365-CAMP.
Finding the campground: Mather Campground is located across from the visitor center in Grand Canyon Village.

Description: The park's main campground, it is centrally located in Grand Canyon Village. Shuttle service is available in the village all year, and along West Rim Drive in summer. There are hiking trails along the canyon rim and into the gorge. During the season, the campground fills early. Lodging, restaurants, a supermarket, and a service station are nearby. Ground and air tours are available. The nearest full services are in Williams and Flagstaff.

2 Trailer Village

Location: Grand Canyon Village.
Sites: 78 RV with full hookups.
Road conditions: Paved.
Management: Grand Canyon National Park, 520-638-7808, 303-297-2757.
Finding the campground: Trailer Village is located across from the visitor center in Grand Canyon Village.

Description: Trailer Village is centrally located in Grand Canyon Village, which has lodging, restaurants, a supermarket, and a service station. The nearest full services are in Williams and Flagstaff.

3 Ten-X

Location: Grand Canyon South Rim.
Sites: 70 tent and RV up to 22 feet. No hookups.
Road conditions: Paved.
Management: Kaibab National Forest, 520-638-2443.
Finding the campground: From Williams, drive north 49 miles on Arizona Highway 64, then turn right at the campground sign. The campground is 2.5 miles south of Tusayan.

Changing light reveals a different Grand Canyon, depending on the day and the hour.

Description: This Forest Service campground is a good alternative to camping in Grand Canyon National Park, which is 4 miles north. During September, it is a good place to sleep after Grand Canyon Music Festival concerts on the South Rim, and you also have a good chance of hearing elk bugle here. The campground features a nature trail, and group campsites are available. Lodging, restaurants, service stations, and supplies are available in Tusayan and Grand Canyon Village. The nearest full services are in Williams and Flagstaff.

4 Desert View

Location: Grand Canyon South Rim.
Sites: 50 tent and RV sites. No hookups.
Road conditions: Paved.
Management: Grand Canyon National Park, 520-638-7808.
Finding the campground: From Grand Canyon Village, drive 25 miles east on East Rim Drive to Desert View. From Cameron on U.S. Highway 89, drive west 32 miles on Arizona Highway 64. The campground is 0.25 mile north of the East Entrance Station.

Description: Desert View is famous for its unique view of Grand Canyon, the Colorado River, and the Painted Desert to the east. The small village has minimal services—a snack bar, service station, and limited supplies. The nearest full services are in Flagstaff.

WILLIAMS

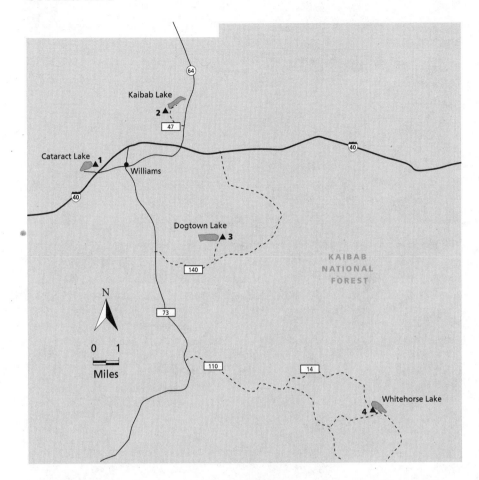

The town of Williams, "Gateway to the Grand Canyon," was named for mountain man Bill Williams. Its Western heritage is evident along its historic main street. Located on the high, cool Coconino Plateau, Williams and the surrounding area are popular summer recreation destinations. Grand Canyon Railroad offers an opportunity to ride a steam train to Grand Canyon. Several reservoirs supply water for the town and boating and fishing for recreationists. Three hiking trails lead to the summit of Bill Williams Mountain, just south of town, and the backcountry of Sycamore Canyon Wilderness lies southeast of town, near White Horse Lake.

The Benham Trail winds through towering ponderosa pines on Bill Williams Mountain.

For more information:
Ash Fork Chamber of Commerce
P.O. Box 494
616 Lewis Ave.
Ash Fork, AZ 86320
520-637-2442
520-637-2269
Fax: 520-637-2442

Williams–Forest Service Visitor Center
200 W. Railroad Ave.
P.O. Box 235
Williams, AZ 86046
520-635-4061
Fax: 520-635-1417

WILLIAMS

		Elevation	Season	RV/Trailer	Sites	Drinking Water	Fishing	RV dump	Hiking trails	Boating	Boat launch	Handicap access	Fee ($)	Stay limit (days)
1	Cataract Lake	6,800	May-Oct	•	18	x	•			•	•	•	•	14
2	Kaibab Lake	6,800	May-Oct	•	72	x	•	•		•	•	•	•	14
3	Dogtown Lake	7,000	Apr-Nov	•	51	x	•		•	•	•	•	•	14
4	White Horse Lake	6,600	May-Oct	•	85	x	•			•	•	•	•	14

1 Cataract Lake

Location: Williams.
Sites: 18 tent and RV up to 18 feet. No hookups.
Road conditions: Paved.
Management: Kaibab National Forest, 520-635-4707.
Finding the campground: From Williams, drive west on Bill Williams Avenue, and pass under Interstate 40.

Description: This small campground is convenient to Williams, where full services are available. Boating (limited to 1-hp electric motors) and fishing are popular on the lake. Nearby Bill Williams Mountain has several hiking trails, and miles of forest roads provide opportunities for mountain biking and exploring.

2 Kaibab Lake

Location: Williams.
Sites: 72 tent and RV up to 22 feet. No hookups.
Road conditions: Paved.
Management: Kaibab National Forest, 520-635-4707.
Finding the campground: From Williams, go 1 mile east on Interstate 40, then exit north on Arizona Highway 64. Continue 1 more mile, then turn left on Forest Road 47, and go 1 mile to the campground.

Description: Boating (limited to 1-hp electric motors) and fishing are available on Kaibab Lake. The campground makes a good base for day trips to Grand Canyon National Park, and for exploring the forested Coconino Plateau and the mountains south of Williams. Full services are available in nearby Williams.

3 Dogtown Lake

Location: About 7 miles southeast of Williams, on the Coconino Plateau.
Sites: 51 tent and RV up to 22 feet. No hookups.
Road conditions: Paved and all-weather dirt.
Management: Kaibab National Forest, 520-635-4707.
Finding the campground: From Williams, drive 4 miles south on Perkinsville Road, Forest Road 73, then turn left on Forest Road 140. Go 2.5 miles, then turn left on Forest Road 132 and continue less than a mile to the campground.

Description: Dogtown Lake is popular with both boaters and anglers. The campground has a short nature trail, and a longer hiking trail takes you to the top of Davenport Hill. There are many other hiking trails on nearby Bill Williams Mountain and in Sycamore Canyon Wilderness. The forest road system provides plenty of opportunities for exploring and mountain biking. Full services are available in Williams.

4 White Horse Lake

Location: About 17 miles southeast of Williams, near Sycamore Canyon.
Sites: 85 tent and RV up to 22 feet. No hookups.
Road conditions: Paved and all-weather dirt.
Management: Kaibab National Forest, 520-635-4707.
Finding the campground: From Williams, drive 8 miles south on Perkinsville Road, Forest Road 73, then turn left on Forest Road 110. Go 7 miles, then turn left on Forest Road 109 and go 2 miles to the lake and campground.

Description: White Horse Lake features boating (limited to 1-hp electric motors) and is very popular with anglers. The campground is an ideal base for exploring the western Mogollon Rim country to the south. FR 110 continues south of the campground to Sycamore Point, a dramatic viewpoint overlooking the rugged Sycamore Canyon Wilderness. Miles of other forest roads are great for mountain biking. Full services are available in Williams.

FLAGSTAFF

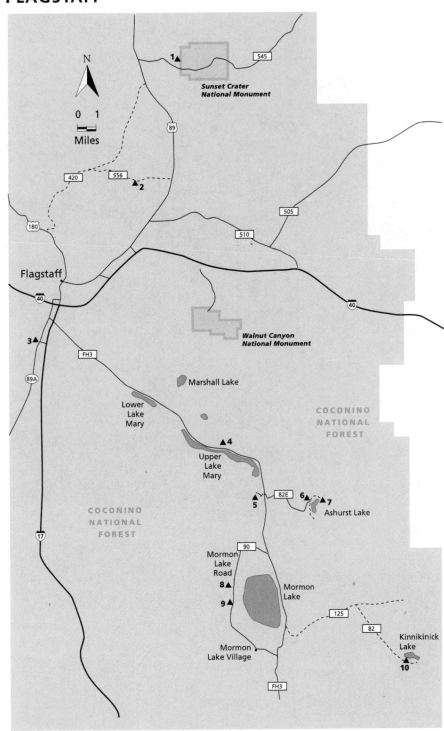

The San Francisco Peaks are Arizona's highest summits.

The largest city in northern Arizona, Flagstaff has a full range of visitor services, as well as cultural events and museums. Spend some time at the Museum of Northern Arizona to learn more about the natural and human history of the area. The Arboretum at Flagstaff has nine gardens that display plants native to the area, including 30 rare and endangered species. Lowell Observatory, from which the planet Pluto was discovered, also has an excellent visitor center.

The Coconino Plateau surrounding Flagstaff is heavily forested with ponderosa pine. The high-mountain elevation provides a welcome respite from the heat of the deserts below. The highest mountains in the state, the San Francisco Peaks, dominate the skyline to the north. The majestic summits are home of the gods in both the Navajo and Hopi religions, and are the largest of more than 200 volcanoes in the area. Nearby Sunset Crater National Monument preserves the results of the most recent volcanic eruption. Walnut Canyon and Wupatki National Monuments allow visitors to view ancient dwellings used by the Sinagua Indians, and understand how they lived. Southeast of the city lies a section of the Mogollon Plateau known locally as "Lake Country." Numerous lakes on this high, forested plateau support angling, boating, and other water sports. The plateau ends abruptly at the south-facing escarpment of the Mogollon Rim. Most of the forest is laced with dirt roads, and it is a mountain biker's paradise. There are also miles of hiking trails, the best known of which is the Arizona Trail, which traverses the plateau on its way from Utah to Mexico.

For more information:
Flagstaff Convention & Visitors Bureau
211 W. Aspen Ave.
Flagstaff, AZ 86001
520-779-7611
Fax: 520-556-1305

FLAGSTAFF

		Elevation	Season	RV/Trailer	Sites	Drinking Water	Fishing	RV dump	Hiking trails	Boating	Boat launch	Handicap access	Fee ($)	Stay limit (days)
1	Bonito	6,900	Apr-Oct	•	44	•			•			•	•	14
2	Little Elden Springs Horse Camp	7,200	May-Sep	•	15	•							•	14
3	Fort Tuthill County Park	6,900	May-Sep	•	75	•			•			•	•	14
4	Lakeview	6,900	May-Sep	•	30	•	•			•			•	14
5	Pinegrove	6,900	May-Sep	•	46	•	•	•		•			•	14
6	Ashurst Lake	7,000	May-Sep	•	35	•	•			•	•		•	14
7	Forked Pine	7,100	May-Sep	•	33	•	•			•			•	14
8	Dairy Springs	7,000	May-Sep	•	27	•	•		•	•			•	14
9	Double Springs	7,000	May-Sep	•	16	•	•		•	•			•	14
10	Kinnikinick	7,000	May-Sep	•	18		•			•	•		•	14

1 Bonito

Location: About 16 miles north of Flagstaff, near Sunset Crater National Monument.
Sites: 44 tent and RV up to 22 feet. No hookups.
Road conditions: Paved.
Management: Coconino National Forest, 520-526-0866.
Finding the campground: From Flagstaff, drive about 14 miles north on U.S. Highway 89, then turn right on the Sunset Crater road, Forest Road 545. Go 2 miles, then turn left into the campground.

Description: Bonito Campground is named after the nearby Bonito Lava Flow, which erupted from the base of Sunset Crater Volcano less than 1,000 years ago. The campground is in an open stand of ponderosa pines in a lunarlike landscape—a great place to watch the full moon rise. The nearby Park Service visitor center explains the volcanic history of the area. Naturalist programs are available. Several trails provide access to viewpoints and natural features. Wupatki National Monument is 16 miles north. It features ruins from a Native American culture that thrived in the area northeast of Sunset Crater. The nearest full services are in Flagstaff.

2 Little Elden Springs Horse Camp

Location: About 7 miles north of Flagstaff, at the base of Mount Elden.
Sites: 15 tent and RV up to 35 feet. No hookups.
Road conditions: Dirt.
Management: Coconino National Forest, 520-526-0866.
Finding the campground: From Flagstaff, drive about 5 miles north on U.S. Highway 89, then turn left on Forest Road 556. Continue 2 miles to the campground.

Description: Though open to all, this is a campground with facilities for equestrians. It is ideally placed at a trailhead for the extensive Mount Elden–Dry Lake Hills trail system. The campground is in a pleasant stand of ponderosa pine and gambel oak below the 2,000-foot east slopes of Mount Elden. The nearest full services are in Flagstaff.

3 Fort Tuthill County Park

Location: Flagstaff.
Sites: 75 tent and RV. No hookups.
Road conditions: Paved.
Management: Coconino County Parks and Recreation, 520-774-3464.
Finding the campground: From Flagstaff, drive 2 miles south on Interstate 17, then exit at Arizona Highway 89A. Turn right (west) into the park and campground.

Description: Site of the annual Coconino County Fair and numerous other events, the park features the campground, picnic areas, and a country store. Full services are available in Flagstaff.

4 Lakeview

Location: About 11 miles southeast of Flagstaff, on Upper Lake Mary.
Sites: 30 tent and RV up to 26 feet. No hookups.
Road conditions: Paved.
Management: Coconino National Forest, 520-774-1147.
Finding the campground: From Flagstaff, drive 11 miles southeast on Lake Mary Road, Forest Highway 3, and turn left into the campground.

Description: Fishing and boating on Upper Lake Mary are two of this scenic, pine-forested campground's attractions. Full services are available in Flagstaff, and there are limited supplies at the north end of Lower Lake Mary 6 miles north. Both lakes are good sites for wildlife viewing, including migrating waterfowl, bald eagles, and resident osprey. Elk are common in the area also.

5 Pinegrove

Location: About 16 miles southeast of Flagstaff, near Upper Lake Mary.
Sites: 46 tent and RV up to 45 feet. No hookups.
Road conditions: Paved.
Management: Coconino National Forest, 520-774-1147.
Finding the campground: From Flagstaff, drive 16 miles southeast on Lake Mary Road, Forest Highway 3, and turn right on Forest Road 651. Continue 0.5 mile to the campground.

Description: Located in northern Arizona's pine-forested lake country, the campground can serve as a base for trips to most of the lakes in the area. Left over from the last ice age, many of the natural lakes on this high plateau have been augmented with small dams. Limited services are available at Mormon Lake Village, 10 miles south, while full services are available in Flagstaff.

6 Ashurst Lake

Location: About 21 miles southeast of Flagstaff, on Ashurst Lake.
Sites: 35 tent and RV up to 35 feet. No hookups.
Road conditions: Paved.
Management: Coconino National Forest, 520-774-1147.
Finding the campground: From Flagstaff, drive 16 miles southeast on Lake Mary Road, Forest Highway 3, and turn left (east) on Ashurst Lake Road, Forest Road 82E. Continue 5 miles to the campground.

Description: Ashurst Lake is popular with boaters and anglers. Because the lake tends to be breezy, it is a destination for sailboarders as well. It is also a

Alpine tundra at 11,000 feet on Agassiz Peak.

great place to view wildlife, including waterfowl, hawks, and songbirds. The duck watching is especially good—it's a real quack fest. The campground is on Anderson Mesa in an open forest of ponderosa pine, pinyon pine, and juniper. Limited services are available at Mormon Lake Village, 15 miles south, while full services are available in Flagstaff.

7 Forked Pine

Location: About 22 miles southeast of Flagstaff, on Ashurst Lake.
Sites: 33 tent and RV up to 26 feet. No hookups.
Road conditions: Paved.
Management: Coconino National Forest, 520-774-1147.
Finding the campground: From Flagstaff, drive 16 miles southeast on Lake Mary Road, Forest Highway 3, and turn left on Ashurst Lake Road, Forest Road 82E. Continue 6 miles to the campground.

Description: This is the second campground at Ashurst Lake, located on the northeast shore.

8 Dairy Springs

Location: About 24 miles southeast of Flagstaff, on Mormon Lake.
Sites: 27 tent and RV up to 35 feet. No hookups.
Road conditions: Paved.
Management: Coconino National Forest, 520-774-1147.
Finding the campground: From Flagstaff, drive 20 miles southeast on Lake Mary Road, Forest Highway 3, then turn right on Mormon Lake Road, Forest Road 90. Continue 4 miles to the campground, which is on the right.

Description: The campground is located in a stand of ponderosa pines across the road from Mormon Lake, the largest natural lake in Arizona. Most of the year, the lake is actually a shallow marsh, but that makes it a prime spot for wildlife viewing. In addition, several trails start from the campground and lead to scenic overlooks. Group camping is available. Mormon Lake has limited fishing. Some supplies and a restaurant are in Mormon Lake Village, 4 miles south. Full services are available in Flagstaff.

9 Double Springs

Location: About 25 miles southeast of Flagstaff, on Mormon Lake.
Sites: 16 tent and RV up to 35 feet. No hookups.
Road conditions: Paved.
Management: Coconino National Forest, 520-774-1147.
Finding the campground: From Flagstaff, drive 20 miles southeast on Lake Mary Road, Forest Highway 3, then turn right on Mormon Lake Road, Forest Road 90. Continue 5 miles to the campground, which is on the right.

Description: This campground is just down the road from Dairy Springs Campground, and is also across the road from Mormon Lake, in tall pines. Mormon Lake has limited fishing. A short hiking trail leads to a rock ledge with a good view of Mormon Lake. Some supplies and a restaurant are in Mormon Lake Village, 3 miles south. Full services are available in Flagstaff.

10 Kinnikinick

Location: About 35 miles southeast of Flagstaff, at Kinnikinick Lake.
Sites: 18 tent and RV up to 22 feet. No hookups.
Road conditions: Dirt.
Management: Coconino National Forest, 520-774-1147.
Finding the campground: From Flagstaff, drive 25 miles southeast on Lake Mary Road, Forest Highway 3, then turn left on FR 125. Go 5 miles, then turn right on FR 82, the main road. Continue another 5 miles to the campground, which is on the left.

Description: The campground is on the shore of Kinnikinick Lake, on a high grassy plateau with scattered ponderosa pines, pinyon pine, and junipers. As with the other lakeside campgrounds, this is a good spot for wildlife viewing, including bald eagles, elk, and antelope. Limited services are available at Mormon Lake Village; the nearest full services are in Flagstaff.

Indian Country

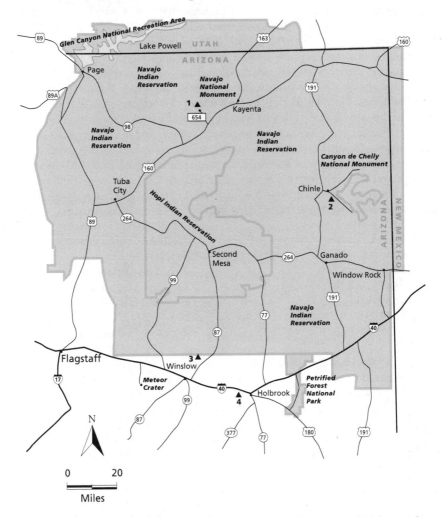

Indian Country is a vast and colorful land, a part of the Colorado Plateau bordered on the north by Lake Powell and the San Juan River, on the west by Grand Canyon, on the east by New Mexico, and on the south by Interstate 40. It is the home of the Navajo Nation, which is the largest Indian reservation in the United States, covering one-sixth of Arizona and extending into three neighboring states. Many Navajo still live as herders of sheep, goats, cattle, and horses. Although most Navajo families live in modern houses, some still live in the traditional mud and wood hogans.

The plateau is also the home of the Hopi Tribe, which occupies villages on spectacular mesas. One of the Hopi towns, Old Oraibi, is the oldest continuously occupied settlement in North America. The Hopi still practice traditional religious ceremonies. The kachina dances take place January through July, and some of them are open to the public.

Lake Powell, one of the most popular attractions in the National Park Service system, draws 3.5 million visitors annually. Often described as "a Grand Canyon with water," Lake Powell is 186 miles long with 1,960 miles of shoreline. It features orange sandstone cliffs interspersed with sandy beaches and, at 3,700 feet, the area gets sunshine 78 percent of the time. Its prime geological attraction is the world-famous Rainbow Bridge National Monument.

Ruins and artifacts from the Anasazi culture, which thrived in northeast Arizona until about 1,000 years ago, are preserved at Navajo National Monument. Petrified Forest National Park preserves one of the largest exposures of petrified wood in the world. The park's soft, rolling hills of pastel-colored shale positively glow with color just after sunrise or before sunset, and are appropriately called the "Painted Desert."

Near Winslow, a giant meteorite smashed into the earth 22,000 years ago, blasting out a crater nearly a mile across. Meteor Crater is one of the best preserved craters on earth and was used by NASA to train lunar astronauts. You can view Meteor Crater from the modern visitor center on its north rim.

For more information:

Holbrook/Petrified Chamber of Commerce
100 E. Arizona St.
Holbrook, AZ 86025
520-524-6558
800-524-2459
Fax: 520-524-1719

Joseph City Chamber of Commerce
242 N. Westover
P.O. Box 36
Joseph City, AZ 86032

Navajo Nation Tourism Office
P.O. Box 663
Window Rock, AZ 85615
520-871-6659
Fax: 520-871-7381

Page/Lake Powell Chamber of Commerce
106 S. Lake Powell Blvd.
P.O. Box 727
Page, AZ 86040
520-645-2741
Fax: 520-645-3181

Winslow Chamber of Commerce
P.O. Box 460
300 W. North Rd.
Winslow, AZ 86047
520-289-2434
Fax: 520-289-5660

INDIAN COUNTRY

		Elevation	Season	RV/Trailer	Sites	Drinking Water	Fishing	RV dump	Hiking trails	Boating	Boat launch	Handicap access	Fee ($)	Stay limit (days)
1	Betatakin	7,300	May-Oct	•	30				•					7
2	Cottonwood	5,500	All year	•	104	•		•	•				•	14
3	Homolovi Ruins	4,850	All year	•	61	•		•	•			•	•	14
4	Cholla Lake	5,000	All year	•	15	•	•			•	•		•	14

1 Betatakin

Location: About 40 miles southwest of Kayenta, at Navajo National Monument.
Sites: 30 tent and RV. No hookups.
Road conditions: Paved.
Management: Navajo National Monument, 520-672-2366.
Finding the campground: From Kayenta, drive 29 miles southwest on U.S. Highway 160, then turn right onto Arizona Highway 564. (This junction is 54 miles northeast of Tuba City.) Continue 10 miles to the visitor center and campground.

Description: The campground is located in a pinyon pine and juniper forest near the rim of Tsegi Canyon. Navajo National Monument, located within the Navajo Indian Reservation, protects a number of ruins that were occupied by the Anasazi 1,000 years ago. The visitor center is a good place to learn about this tenacious Southwestern culture. This unit of the monument encompasses two of the most famous ruins. Betatakin Ruin is visible from a nearby overlook and can be hiked to via a 5-mile round trip. Keet Seel ruin is accessible via a longer trail, best done as an overnight hike; access is limited by permit in order to protect the fragile ruins. The nearest services are in Kayenta; full services are available in Page and Flagstaff.

The snowcapped summits of the San Francisco Peaks form the backdrop to Wukoki Ruin.

2 Cottonwood

Location: Near Chinle, at Canyon de Chelly National Monument.
Sites: 104 tent and RV up to 34 feet. No hookups.
Road conditions: Paved.
Management: Canyon de Chelly National Monument, 520-674-5510.
Finding the campground: From the junction of U.S. Highway 191 and Tribal Road 64, go 3 miles east on TR 64, through Chinle, past the monument visitor center, then turn right and go 0.5 mile to the campground.

Description: Cottonwood Campground is a fine base for exploring Canyon del Muerto and Canyon de Chelly, the two beautiful canyons that make up the national monument. Paved roads follow the rims of each canyon. A spectacular foot trail leads to the famous White House Ruin. Other canyon bottom exploration is available on trips with Navajo guides. Group camping is available by reservation. The campground is within walking distance of the cafeteria at Thunderbird Lodge. Cottonwood Campground may be transferred to the Navajo National Parks and Recreation Department for management in the spring of 1999. Please contact the park for further information. Limited services are available in Chinle; the nearest full services are in Gallup, New Mexico.

3 Homolovi Ruins

Location: About 6 miles east of Winslow, at Homolovi Ruins State Park.
Sites: 61 tent and RV. 1 electric hookup.
Road conditions: Paved.
Management: Homolovi Ruins State Park, 520-289-4106.
Finding the campground: From Winslow, go 4 miles east on Interstate 40, then exit at Arizona Highway 87. Turn left, and continue 1 mile north, then turn left and go another mile to the park and campground.

Description: This campground is located in the Painted Desert near the ruins of an ancient Native American community. The state park has a visitor center and interpretive trails. World famous for its ethereal beauty, the Painted Desert is gently rolling plateau country. The multiple pastel colors of the exposed shale and sandstone rocks catch the early morning or late evening light, and provide an ever-changing display of subtle color. Nearby attractions include Meteor Crater, the best preserved impact crater in the world, and Petrified Forest National Park, which protects vast outcrops of fossilized wood. Full services are available 6 miles west in Winslow.

4 Cholla Lake

Location: About 10 miles west of Holbrook.
Sites: 15 tent and RV. Some partial hookups.
Road conditions: Paved.
Management: Navajo Country Recreation Department, 520-524-6161.

Finding the campground: From Winslow, go 23 miles east on Interstate 40 (from Holbrook, go 8 miles west on I-40); exit at Joseph City (Exit 277). Go south, then almost immediately turn left (east) onto the park access road and continue 2 miles to the campground.

Description: The campground's main attraction is its convenient location near the interstate. Fishing and boating are available on the lake. Nearby attractions include the historic downtown section of Holbrook, and Petrified Forest National Park. Full services are available in Holbrook, 10 miles east.

River Country

Lake Mead

Hoover Dam

Colorado River

Lake Mead National Recreation Area

93

NEVADA

68

Bullhead City

Kingman

40

95

Lake Havasu City

93

Colorado River

CALIFORNIA

ARIZONA

Parker

95

72

60

Quartzite

10

Colorado River

Kofa National Wildlife Refuge

95

8

Yuma

ARIZONA

MEXICO

Cabeza Prieta National Wildlife Refuge

N

0   20

Miles

The expansive western deserts and mountains of the state are bordered on the west by the Colorado River, the defining feature of this landscape. A string of dams impounds the waters of the river, creating Lake Mead, Lake Mohave, Lake Havasu, and Imperial Reservoir, which provide almost unlimited water recreation. Several national wildlife refuges along the river provide excellent opportunities to observe wildlife. Most of the region's campgrounds are found along the river and its lakes. But do not ignore the desert. There is a great variety of desert backcountry and wilderness to explore. The BLM and the state parks system provide a number of campgrounds, and the sheer vastness of the public lands means you can enjoy dispersed camping in complete solitude if you desire. (Though this FalconGuide covers only the campgrounds on the Arizona side of the river, you will find more facilities and long-term visitor areas on the California side.)

KINGMAN

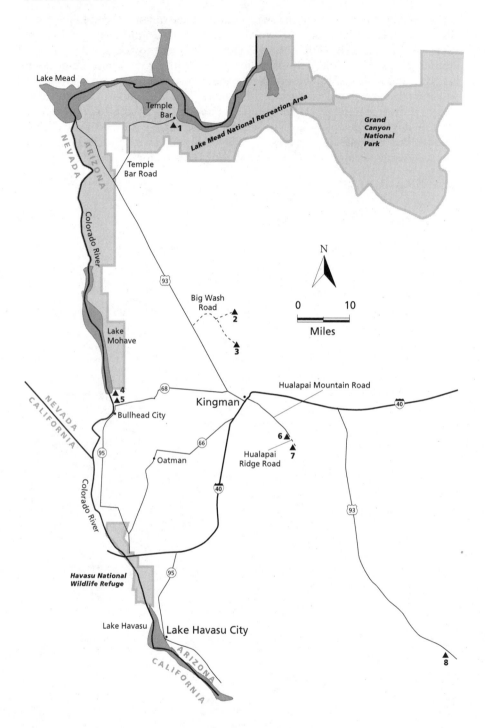

Lake Mead

Temple
Bar
▲1

Lake Mead National Recreation Area

Grand
Canyon
National
Park

NEVADA

ARIZONA

Colorado River

Temple
Bar Road

93

Big Wash
Road
▲2

▲3

N

0   10

Miles

Lake
Mohave

NEVADA

CALIFORNIA

▲4
▲5

68

Kingman

Hualapai Mountain Road

40

Bullhead City

Colorado River

66

6 ▲

▲7

Oatman

Hualapai
Ridge Road

40

93

Havasu National
Wildlife Refuge

95

95

Lake Havasu

Lake Havasu City

ARIZONA

▲8

CALIFORNIA

Kingman, on Interstate 40 and historic Route 66, is the jumping off point for the northern portion of River Country. When the Colorado River leaves the Grand Canyon at the Grand Wash Cliffs, it's impounded in Lake Mead, the huge reservoir formed behind Hoover Dam. The lake makes a sharp turn from west to south, and defines the northwest corner of the state. Lake Mead is an angler's paradise and is a very popular water sports playground as well. Sailing is great fun on the wide-open expanses of the lake, and you can water ski, scuba dive, and even sea kayak. If you like to explore the backcountry, there are several challenging wilderness areas scattered along the desert mountain ranges east of the river. South of Kingman, the Hualapai Mountains rise to over 8,000 feet and provide a cool, forested escape from the desert. In Bullhead City, on the Arizona side of the river below Davis Dam, learn about the history of the river and its exploration at the Colorado River Museum. Near Bullhead City is the ghost town of Oatman. Once a busy mining town, Oatman is famous for the wild burros that still wander its streets.

For more information:

Bullhead City Chamber of
Commerce
1251 Hwy. 95
Bullhead City, AZ 86429
520-754-4121
Fax: 520-754-5514

Chloride Chamber of Commerce
P.O. Box 545
Chloride, AZ 86431
520-565-3210

Dolan Springs Chamber of
Commerce
P.O. Box 274
Dolan Springs, AZ 86441
520-767-3530

Golden Valley Chamber of
Commerce
505 Hwy. 68
P.O. Box 10300
Kingman, AZ 86401
520-565-3311

Mohave Valley Chamber of
Commerce
P.O. Box 9101
Ft. Mohave, AZ 86427
520-768-2777
Fax: 520-768-3371

Oatman-Goldroad Chamber of
Commerce
P.O. Box 64
Oatman, AZ 86433
520-768-4871

Granite cliffs frame the view from the Hualapai Mountains.

KINGMAN

		Elevation	Season	RV/Trailer	Sites	Drinking Water	Fishing	RV dump	Hiking trails	Boating	Boat launch	Handicap access	Fee ($)	Stay limit (days)
1	Temple Bar	1,400	All year	•	152	•	•	•	•	•	•	•	•	30
2	Windy Point	5,000	May-Oct		7								•	14
3	Packsaddle	5,000	May-Oct		4									14
4	Katherine Landing	700	All year	•	162	•	•	•	•	•	•		•	30
5	Davis County Park	700	All year	•	175	•	•	•		•	•		•	14
6	Hualapai Mountain Park	6,200	All year	•	81	•			•				•	14
7	Wild Cow Springs	6,500	May-Oct	•	24				•			•	•	14
8	Burro Creek	2,000	All year	•	30	•	•	•				•	•	14

1 Temple Bar

Location: About 80 miles north of Kingman, on Lake Mead.
Sites: 152 tent and RV. No hookups.
Road conditions: Paved.
Management: Lake Mead National Recreation Area, 702-293-8907, 702-293-8990.
Finding the campground: From Kingman, go 54 miles north on U.S. Highway 93, then turn right on Temple Bar Road. Continue 26 miles to Temple Bar.

Description: The campground is located on Lake Mead in the Mohave Desert. The lake offers fishing for largemouth bass, striped bass, rainbow trout, channel catfish, crappie, and bluegill. Boating, including sailing, kayaking, and canoeing, are popular on the lake. Water skiing, sailboarding, scuba diving, and snorkeling are also popular. Boat rental and a full-service marina are located in Temple Bar. The nearest full services are in Kingman.

2 Windy Point

Location: About 34 miles north of Kingman, in the Cerbat Mountains.
Sites: 7 tent.
Road conditions: Paved, dirt.
Management: Bureau of Land Management, 520-692-4400.
Finding the campground: From Kingman, drive 20 miles north on U.S. Highway 93, then turn right on Big Wash Road. Continue 11 miles east to the campground.

Description: This small campground is set in the rugged Cerbat Mountains, a high desert range studded with pinyon pines and juniper trees. It's a good base for exploring the mountains, including the nearby Mount Tipton Wilderness. The nearest full services are in Kingman.

Stark desert and rock pinnacles in the Mohave Desert above the Colorado River.

3 Packsaddle

Location: About 33 miles north of Kingman, in the Cerbat Mountains.
Sites: 4 tent.
Road conditions: Paved, dirt.
Management: Bureau of Land Management, 520-692-4400.
Finding the campground: From Kingman, drive 20 miles north on U.S. Highway 93, then turn right on Big Wash Road. Continue 9 miles east to the campground.

Description: This is a small tent-only campground in the Cerbat Mountains. Like nearby Windy Point Campground, it's a good base for exploring the mountains. The nearest full services are in Kingman.

4 Katherine Landing

Location: About 34 miles west of Kingman, on Lake Mohave.
Sites: 162 tent and RV up to 25 feet. No hookups.
Road conditions: Paved.
Management: Lake Mead National Recreation Area, 702-293-8920.
Finding the campground: From Bullhead City, go north about 3 miles on Arizona Highway 68, then turn left at the Katherine Landing sign and go north 3 miles to the campground. This turnoff is 30 miles west of Kingman.

Description: This large campground is in the Mohave Desert on the southeast shore of 67-mile long Lake Mohave. Lake Mohave offers a wide range of boating and water sports, and is fished for trout, catfish, and striped, largemouth, and smallmouth bass. A full-service marina is available, and full services are in Bullhead City.

5 Davis County Park

Location: Bullhead City, on the Colorado River.
Sites: 175 tent and RV. Some partial hookups.
Road conditions: Paved.
Management: Mohave County Park, 520-754-4606
Finding the campground: From Bullhead City on Arizona Highway 95, go north to the park entrance road.

Description: This is a desert campground on the Colorado River below Davis Dam. Hookups are available, as are showers. The river is fished for largemouth and smallmouth bass, as well as other species. Full services are available in Bullhead City.

6 Hualapai Mountain Park

Location: About 13 miles southeast of Kingman, in the Hualapai Mountains.
Sites: 81 tent and RV.
Road conditions: Paved.
Management: Hualapai Mountain Park, 520-757-3859.
Finding the campground: From Kingman, go 13 miles southeast on Stockton Hill–Hualapai Mountain Road to the park.

Description: The campground and park are located in granite and pine country in the Hualapai Mountains, high above the hot Mohave Desert. Some hookups are available. The Hualapai Mountain Trail is popular with hikers. Backcountry hikers can explore the nearby Wabayuma Peak Wilderness, which is further south along the crest. Full services are available in Kingman.

7 Wild Cow Springs

Location: About 19 miles southeast of Kingman, in the Hualapai Mountains.
Sites: 24 tent and RV. No hookups.
Road conditions: Paved, dirt.
Management: Bureau of Land Management, 520-692-4400.
Finding the campground: From Kingman, go 14 miles southeast on Stockton Hill–Hualapai Mountain Road, then continue 5 miles on Hualapai Ridge Road.

Description: This campground is located high in the rugged Hualapai Mountains, a pine-forested island in the surrounding Mohave Desert. It's not only a good escape from the hot desert but also is a starting point for exploring the mountains, including Wayabuma Peak Wilderness to the south. There are several hiking trails in the Hualapai Peak and Wabayuma Peak areas. Full services are available in Kingman.

8 Burro Creek

Location: About 68 miles southeast of Kingman, on Burro Creek.
Sites: 30 tent and RV. No hookups.
Road conditions: Paved.
Management: Bureau of Land Management, 520-692-4400.
Finding the campground: From Kingman, go 22 miles east on Interstate 40, then turn south on U.S. Highway 93. Continue 46 miles to the campground, which is on the right.

Description: This desert campground is a popular winter spot, but a bit hot in summer. It is a good base for exploring several nearby backcountry areas, including Burro Creek, Arrastra Mountain, and Aubrey Peak Wildernesses. Full services are available in Kingman, 68 miles north, and Wickenburg, 60 miles south.

LAKE HAVASU

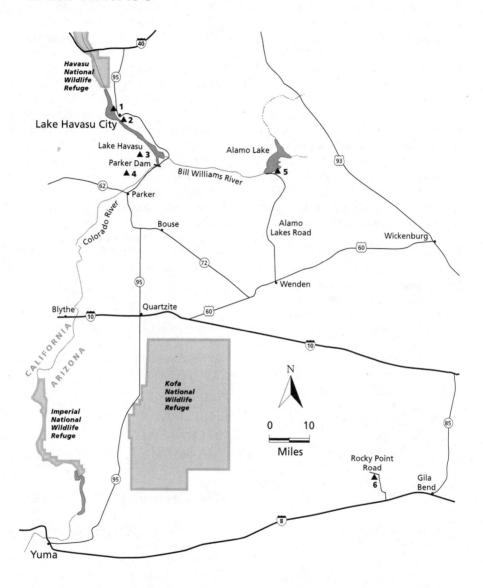

Lake Havasu is famous as the site of London Bridge, but there is more to this central section of River Country than transplanted bridges. The upper end of the lake is in Havasu National Wildlife Refuge, a haven for waterfowl and a paddler's paradise. Boaters, sailors, anglers, and other water sports enthusiasts, all enjoy the impounded waters of the lake, formed by Parker Dam. There are campgrounds along the lakeshore and the river, above and below the dam. A tributary of the Colorado, the Bill Williams River, has been dammed to create Alamo

Lake. The state park here is a good jumping off point for exploring the nearby desert wilderness areas. Cultural attractions include the Creative Cultural Center in Lake Havasu City, where year-round events feature Native American and Southwestern arts and crafts, traditional dancing, and storytelling. You can also visit the tribal museum on the Colorado River Indian Reservation, just south of Parker. It represents the Navajo, Hopi, Mohave, and Chemehuevi tribes.

The southern section of River Country is anchored by the sunny city of Yuma. Located near the Mexican border in the lowest part of the state, Yuma offers warm winters and desert hiking as well as opportunities for water sports and fishing. Cultural attractions include a number of museums and Yuma Territorial Prison State Historic Park. Inland, the desert town of Quartzsite is a winter mecca for RVers escaping colder climates, and for rockhounds who are attracted to the gem and mineral shows. The Kofa National Wildlife Refuge is a preserve established to protect the majestic desert bighorn sheep, and is an interesting and challenging wilderness to explore. In the Kofa Mountains, Palm Canyon is the site of the only native palm trees in Arizona.

There are few public campgrounds, but the BLM has designated several long-term visitor areas in the desert, so there are plenty of places to camp. If you want to escape the crowds, dispersed camping is allowed on most of the public land in southwest Arizona.

For more information:

Bouse Chamber of Commerce
P.O. Box 696
Bouse, AZ 85325
520-851-2391

Ehrenberg Chamber of Commerce
P.O. Box 800
Ehrenberg, AZ 85334
520-923-9601
Fax: 520-923-9602

Gila Bend Chamber of Commerce
P.O. Box A
644 W. Pima
Gila Bend, AZ 85337
520-683-2002
Fax: 602-256-7856

Lake Havasu City Visitor &
Convention Bureau
1930 Mesquite Ave. #3
Lake Havasu City, AZ 86403
520-855-4115
800-242-8278
Fax: 520-680-0010

McMullen Valley Chamber of
Commerce
P.O. Box 477
Salome, AZ 85348
520-859-3846

Parker Area Chamber of
Commerce
1217 California Ave.
P.O. Box 627
Parker, AZ 85344
520-669-2174
Fax: 520-669-6304

Quartzsite Chamber of Commerce
P.O. Box 85/Hwy. 95
Palm Plaza
Quartzsite, AZ 85346
520-927-5600

City of Somerton
City Manager
Box 638
Somerton, AZ 85350
520-627-8866

Welton Chamber of Commerce
P.O. Box 455
Welton, AZ 85356
520-785-9651

Yuma Convention & Visitors
Bureau & Chamber of Commerce
488 S. Maiden Lane
P.O. Box 10831
Yuma, AZ 85366-8831
520-783-0071
Fax: 520-783-1897

LAKE HAVASU AREA

		Elevation	Season	RV/Trailer	Sites	Drinking Water	Fishing	RV dump	Hiking trails	Boating	Boat launch	Handicap access	Fee ($)	Stay limit (days)
1	Lake Havasu	450	All year	•	74	•	•	•	•	•	•	•	•	14
2	Cattail Cove	480	All year	•	40	•	•	•	•	•	•	•	•	14
3	Buckskin Mountain	420	All year	•	126	•	•	•	•	•	•	•	•	14
4	La Paz County Park	400	All year	•	99	•	•	•		•	•		•	14
5	Alamo Lake State Park	1,250	All year	•	394	•	•	•	•	•	•	•	•	14
6	Painted Rock Petroglyph	800	All year	•	30									

1 Lake Havasu

Location: Lake Havasu City, on Lake Havasu.
Sites: 74 tent and RV. No hookups.
Road conditions: Paved.
Management: Lake Havasu State Park, 520-855-2784.
Finding the campground: The park is just north of London Bridge off London Bridge Road.

Description: This state park on Windsor Beach is a popular water sports destination, some boat-only campsites are available. The lake is fished for striped bass, largemouth bass, and carp. Showers are available. A group campsite is available by reservation. The campground is also a good base for exploring the Havasu Wilderness and the Needles area to the north. Full services are available in Lake Havasu City.

2 Cattail Cove

Location: About 10 miles south of Lake Havasu City, on Lake Havasu.
Sites: 40 tent and RV. Water and electric hookups.
Road conditions: Paved.
Management: Lake Havasu State Park, 520-855-1223.
Finding the campground: From Lake Havasu City, drive south about 10 miles on Arizona Highway 95, then turn right into the park.

Description: In addition to the auto campsites, 25 boat-only campsites are available. Hookups and showers are available. Limited supplies are available near the park; full services are available in Lake Havasu City.

3 Buckskin Mountain

Location: About 11 miles northeast of Parker, on the Colorado River.
Sites: 126 tent and RV. 68 water and electric, 21 electric, 9 full hookups.
Road conditions: Paved.
Management: Buckskin Mountain State Park, 520-667-3231.
Finding the campground: From Parker, go north about 11 miles on Arizona Highway 95 to the park turnoff on the left.

Description: Some hookups are available; the campground has showers, grass, and shade trees. There are several scenic hiking trails. The river is fished for largemouth and striped bass, as well as crappie, sunfish, and channel catfish. Limited services are available nearby, and full services are available in Parker.

4 La Paz County Park

Location: About 8 miles northeast of Parker, on the Colorado River.
Sites: 99 tent and RV. Electric hookups.
Road conditions: Paved.
Management: La Paz County Park, 520-667-2069.
Finding the campground: From Parker, go about 8 miles north on Arizona Highway 95, then turn left into the campground.

Description: This section of the river is a prime spot for waterskiing. Some sites have hookups and sun shelters, and there are beach campsites. Limited services are available nearby, and full services are available in Parker.

5 Alamo Lake

Location: About 86 miles northwest of Wickenburg, at Alamo Lake.
Sites: 394 tent and RV. Some electric hookups.
Road conditions: Paved.
Management: Alamo Lake State Park, 520-669-2088.
Finding the campground: From Wickenburg, go 52 miles west on U.S. Highway 60 to Wenden, then turn right (north) on Alamo Lake Road. Continue 34 miles north to the park.

Description: An out-of-the-way but popular area, Alamo Lake is a flood control basin. The lake is fished for largemouth bass, channel and flathead catfish, tilapia, bullhead, carp, and sunfish. Some campsites have hookups; showers are available, as is a group camp area. Limited services are available in Wenden; full services are available in Parker and Wickenburg.

The rugged and remote Eagletail Mountains are one of many desert ranges in western Arizona's River Country.

6 | Painted Rock Petroglyph

Location: About 31 miles northwest of Gila Bend.
Sites: 30 tent and RV. No hookups.
Road conditions: Dirt.
Management: Bureau of Land Management, 602-780-8090.
Finding the campground: From Gila Bend, go about 16 miles west on Interstate 8 to the Painted Rock interchange, then north 15 miles on Rocky Point Road.

Description: The campground is in the desert near Painted Rock Reservoir, a flood control basin on the Gila River. The rugged Gila Bend Mountains, which include the Woolsey Peak and Signal Peak Wildernesses, lie to the north. The campground's main feature is Hohokam rock art. The historic Mormon Battalion Trail and the Butterfield Stage Route pass through this area. The nearest full services are 31 miles east in Gila Bend.

Central Territory

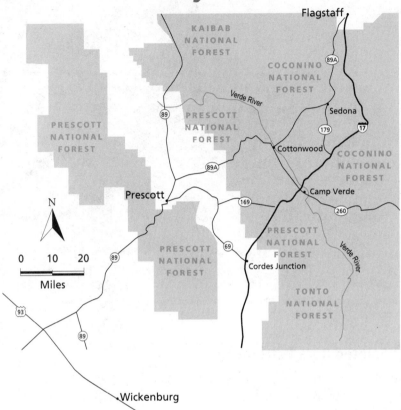

Central Arizona is a land of rugged, pine-forested mountains with a colorful history. The city of Prescott was the territorial capitol before Arizona became a state in 1912, and still has a flavor of those days. Nearby, the Bradshaw Mountains were a major mining center and the site of several large boom towns. The winding Senator Highway, a dirt road, runs the length of the Bradshaws. Still interesting to explore today, 100 years ago it was the main road connecting Arizona Territory's two major cities, Prescott and Tucson. To get a feel for the pioneer days, check out Prescott's Courthouse Plaza and Whiskey Row.

Southwest of Prescott, Wickenburg also has managed to preserve a flavor of the old days. Named after a prosperous gold miner, Wickenburg has long been known for its guest ranches, which vary from simple and plain to truly elegant and fancy. Check out the Desert Caballeros Western Museum, which features cowboy art and displays about Native Americans and pioneer life.

There are plenty of outdoor activities in the Prescott area. Several small lakes attract anglers, and Granite Mountain offers world-class rock climbing. Mountain bikers can explore miles of forest roads and trails. Hikers have several wilderness areas to visit, including the Juniper Mesa, Apache Creek, Granite Mountain, Woodchute, and Castle Creek Wildernesses.

For more information:

Black Canyon City Chamber of
Commerce
P.O. Box 1919
Black Canyon City, AZ 85324
520-374-9797
Fax: 520-374-9225

Chino Valley Chamber of
Commerce
P.O. Box 419
Chino Valley, AZ 86323
520-636-2493

Mayer Area Chamber of
Commerce
Wishbone's Trading & Antique
Store
P.O. Box 248
Hwy. 69
Mayer, AZ 86333-0248
520-632-4355

Prescott Chamber of Commerce
117 W. Goodwin
P.O. Box 1147
Prescott, AZ 86302
520-445-2000
800-266-7534
Fax: 520-445-0068

Prescott Valley Chamber of
Commerce
8307 Hwy. 69, Ste. C
P.O. Box 25357
Prescott Valley, AZ 86312
520-772-8857
Fax: 520-772-4267

Wickenburg Chamber of
Commerce
15 N. Frontier St.
P.O. Drawer CC
Wickenburg, AZ 85358
520-684-5479
800-WICKCHAMBER
Fax: 520-684-5470

PRESCOTT

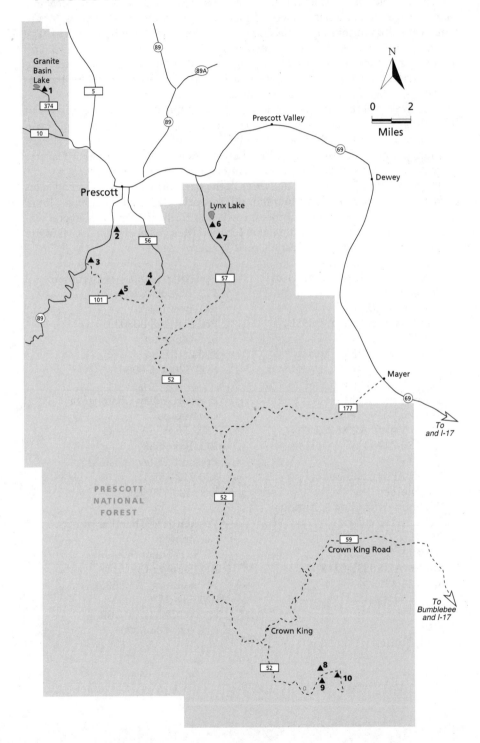

PRESCOTT

		Elevation	Season	RV/Trailer	Sites	Drinking Water	Fishing	RV dump	Hiking trails	Boating	Boat launch	Handicap access	Fee ($)	Stay limit (days)
1	Yavapai	5,600	All year	•	25	•			•			•	•	14
2	White Spar	5,700	All year	•	62	•						•	•	14
3	Indian Creek	5,800	May-Sep	•	27								•	14
4	Groom Creek Horse Camp	6,000	May-Oct	•	37	•			•			•	•	14
5	Lower Wolf Creek	6,000	May-Nov	•	20								•	14
6	Lynx Lake	5,600	Apr-Nov	•	39	•	•		•	•		•	•	7
7	Hilltop	5,700	Apr-Oct	•	38	•	•			•			•	7
8	Hazlett Hollow	6,000	Seasonal	•	15	•	•			•			•	14
9	Turney Gulch	6,000	Seasonal	•	7	•	•		•	•			•	14
10	Kentuck Springs	6,000	Seasonal	•	15		•		•	•			•	14

1 Yavapai

Location: About 8 miles northwest of Prescott, near Granite Mountain.
Sites: 25 tent and RV up to 40 feet. No hookups.
Road conditions: Paved.
Management: Prescott National Forest, 520-445-7253.
Finding the campground: From Prescott, drive west about 4 miles on Iron Springs Road, Forest Road 10, then turn right on Granite Basin Road, Forest Road 374. Continue 2 miles to the campground.

Description: Located near the popular Granite Basin Recreation Area, this campground makes a fine base for exploring Granite Mountain Wilderness. Several hiking trails lead into the wilderness and surrounding country, and to the top of Granite Mountain Wall, which is famous for its world-class rockclimbing. The historical attractions in Prescott are also close at hand. Full services are available in Prescott.

2 White Spar

Location: About 3 miles southwest of Prescott, in the Bradshaw Mountains.
Sites: 62 tent and RV up to 32 feet. No hookups.
Road conditions: Paved, dirt.
Management: Prescott National Forest, 520-445-7253.
Finding the campground: From Prescott, drive about 3 miles south on Arizona Highway 89.

Description: This popular, pine-forested campground is very convenient to Prescott and makes a good starting point for exploring the nearby Bradshaw and Sierra Prieta Mountains. The Sharlot Hall Museum in Prescott is a good place to

An old log cabin in the Bradshaw Mountains southeast of Prescott.

get a feel for life in territorial Arizona, when Prescott was the capital. Full services are available in Prescott.

3 Indian Creek

Location: About 8 miles southwest of Prescott, in the Bradshaw Mountains.
Sites: 27 tent and RV up to 32 feet. No hookups.
Road conditions: Paved.
Management: Prescott National Forest, 520-445-7253.
Finding the campground: From Prescott, drive about 7 miles south on Arizona Highway 89, then turn left on Forest Road 101 and continue 1 mile to the campground.

Description: If you want a remote feeling while still being close to town, this may be the spot for you. The campground makes a good base for exploring the rugged Bradshaw Mountains by mountain bike or vehicle. There are numerous hiking trails in the Bradshaw and Sierra Prieta Mountains. Full services are available in Prescott.

4 Groom Creek Horse Camp

Location: 9 miles south of Prescott, in the Bradshaw Mountains..
Sites: 37 tent and RV up to 35 feet. No hookups.
Road conditions: Paved.

Management: Prescott National Forest, 520-445-7253.
Finding the campground: From Prescott, drive 9 miles south on Forest Road 56.

Description: This is an equestrian camp, and there are several popular horse trails in the nearby forest. The nearest services are in Prescott.

5 Lower Wolf Creek

Location: About 12 miles south of Prescott, in the Bradshaw Mountains.
Sites: 20 tent and RV up to 32 feet. No hookups.
Road conditions: Paved, dirt.
Management: Prescott National Forest, 520-445-7253.
Finding the campground: From Prescott, drive about 10 miles south on Forest Road 56, then turn right onto Forest Road 101. Continue about 2 miles to the campground.

Description: Another out-of-the-way campground that makes a good base for exploring the Bradshaw Mountains, where there are numerous hiking trails and back roads for mountain bikers to explore. Full services are available in Prescott.

6 Lynx Lake

Location: About 5 miles southeast of Prescott, in the Bradshaw Mountains.
Sites: 39 tent and RV up to 32 feet. No hookups.
Road conditions: Paved.
Management: Prescott National Forest, 520-445-7253.
Finding the campground: From Prescott, drive about 3 miles east on Arizona Highway 69 south, then turn right on Walker Road, Forest Road 57. Continue 2 miles to the campground.

Description: With scenic Lynx Lake as a backdrop, this forested campground is one of the nicest in central Arizona. Walker Road continues into the northern Bradshaw Mountains, which you can explore by vehicle or mountain bike. Fishing is very popular here, as is boating (limited to 1-hp electric motors). The nearest full services are in Prescott.

7 Hilltop

Location: 6 miles southeast of Prescott, in the Bradshaw Mountains.
Sites: 38 tent and RV up to 32 feet. No hookups.
Road conditions: Paved.
Management: Prescott National Forest, 520-445-7253.
Finding the campground: From Prescott, drive about 3 miles east on Arizona Highway 69 south, then turn right on Walker Road, Forest Road 57. Continue 3 miles to the campground.

Description: The second campground at Lynx Lake. Prescott has the nearest full services.

8 Hazlett Hollow

Location: About 7 miles southeast of Crown King, in the Bradshaw Mountains.
Sites: 15 tent and RV up to 32 feet. No hookups.
Road conditions: Dirt.
Management: Prescott National Forest, 520-445-7253.
Finding the campground: From Interstate 17 at the junction with Arizona Highway 69, go south on Interstate 17 for 3 miles to the Bloody Basin interchange, then turn right (west). Go 3 miles, then turn left. After another 3 miles, turn right on Crown King Road, Forest Road 59. Continue 16 miles, just past Crown King, then stay left on Forest Road 52. Continue another 7 miles to the campground.

Description: One of three campgrounds in scenic Horsethief Basin, this camp is a good base for exploring the nearby Castle Creek Wilderness. There are a number of hiking trails both inside and outside the wilderness. There is limited fishing and boating on Horsethief Lake. The nearest services are in Crown King, and the nearest full services are in Prescott.

9 Turney Gulch

Location: About 7 miles southeast of Crown King, in the Bradshaw Mountains.
Sites: 7 tent and RV up to 32 feet. No hookups.
Road conditions: Dirt.
Management: Prescott National Forest, 520-445-7253.
Finding the campground: From Interstate 17 at the junction with Arizona Highway 69, go south on Interstate 17 for 3 miles to the Bloody Basin interchange, then turn right (west). Go 3 miles, then turn left. After another 3 miles, turn right on Crown King Road, Forest Road 59. Continue 16 miles, then stay left on Forest Road 52. (This junction is 0.5 mile south of Crown King.) Continue another 7 miles to the campground.

Description: This campground is located in Horsethief Basin near Horsethief Lake, where limited boating and fishing are available. The nearest services are in Crown King; the nearest full services are in Prescott.

10 Kentuck Springs

Location: About 7 miles southeast of Crown King, in the Bradshaw Mountains.
Sites: 15 tent and RV up to 32 feet. No hookups.
Road conditions: Dirt.
Management: Prescott National Forest, 520-445-7253.
Finding the campground: From Interstate 17 at the junction with Arizona Highway 69, go south 3 miles to the Bloody Basin interchange, then turn right

(west). Go 3 miles, then turn left. After another 3 miles, turn right on Crown King Road, Forest Road 59. Continue 16 miles, then stay left on Forest Road 52. (This junction is 0.5 mile south of Crown King.) Continue another 8 miles to the campground.

Description: This campground is located in Horsethief Basin in ponderosa pine forest. A trail leads to Horsethief Lookout, a fire tower on a mountaintop with a panoramic view of much of central Arizona. Limited fishing and boating are available on Horsethief Lake. Crown King has the nearest services, and full services are available in Prescott.

VERDE VALLEY

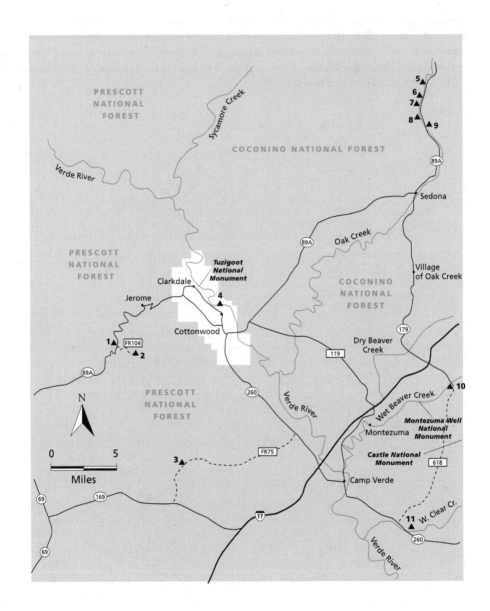

Named by Spanish explorers in the 1540s, the Verde Valley's defining natural feature is the Verde River. Native Americans thrived in the area long before the Europeans arrived, as evidenced by numerous ruins. Two outstanding examples are preserved as national monuments. Tuzigoot National Monument features a hilltop dwelling of many rooms, and Montezuma Castle National Monument protects a multi-story cliff dwelling. Artifacts in these dwellings prove that trade was carried on with peoples from as far away as southern Mexico. There are many other ruins that can be reached by vehicle or foot.

Jerome, on the steep slopes of Mingus Mountain, was the site of one of the richest copper mines in the world. When the mines played out, Jerome nearly became a ghost town. It has since enjoyed a steady revival as an art colony. You can explore the fascinating history of the area at Jerome State Historic Park. Mingus Mountain offers campgrounds in the cool pines at nearly 8,000 feet, and some very scenic hiking trails.

The largest town in the Verde Valley is Cottonwood, a thriving retirement community. Nearby Clarkdale is the terminus for the scenic Verde River Railroad, and also the jumping off point for hikers wanting to investigate the Sycamore Canyon Wilderness. At the lower end of the Verde Valley, the small town of Camp Verde was once a bustling and important military post. Fort Verde State Historic Park preserves some of the original buildings that Army personnel used during the Apache Indian wars. Camp Verde is also the launching point for float trips down the wilderness section of the Verde River.

Snuggled under the red rocks of the Mogollon Rim at the northeast corner of the Verde Valley, Sedona offers numerous art galleries and other southwestern shopping experiences. Sedona is surrounded by national forest and wilderness areas containing some of the most dramatic landscapes in Arizona. One of the most famous is Oak Creek Canyon, which features a rare but accessible permanent stream. You can fish the creek or hike some of the many trails found along the canyon's length, using any of several campgrounds as a base. There are also picnic areas for day use. Other hiking trails penetrate the Red Rock–Secret Mountain, Munds Mountain, Wet Beaver Creek, and Clear Creek Wilderness Areas. There are also miles of trails for mountain bikers.

For more information:

Camp Verde Chamber of
Commerce
435 S. Main St.
P.O. Box 1665
Camp Verde, AZ 86322
520-567-9294

Cottonwood/Verde Valley Chamber
of Commerce
1010 S. Main St.
Cottonwood, AZ 86326
520-634-7593
Fax: 520-634-7594

Clarkdale Chamber of Commerce
P.O. Box 161
Clarkdale, AZ 86324
520-634-3382
Fax: 520-634-0407

Jerome Chamber of Commerce
100 N. Hill St.
P.O. Box K
Jerome, AZ 86331
520-634-2900 or 520-634-5716

Sedona–Oak Creek Canyon
Chamber of Commerce
P.O. Box 478
Arizona Highway 89A & Forest
Sedona, AZ 86336
520-282-7722
800-288-7336
Fax: 520-204-1064

VERDE VALLEY

		Elevation	Season	RV/Trailer	Sites	Drinking Water	Fishing	RV dump	Hiking trails	Boating	Boat launch	Handicap access	Fee ($)	Stay limit (days)
1	Potato Patch	7,000	May-Oct	•	35				•				•	14
2	Mingus Mountain	7,600	May-Oct	•	24				•				•	14
3	Powell Springs	5,300	All year	•	10								•	14
4	Dead Horse Ranch	3,300	All year	•	81	•	•	•				•	•	14
5	Pine Flat	5,500	Jun-Aug	•	58	•	•		•			•	•	7
6	Cave Spring	5,400	Jun-Aug	•	78	•	•		•			•	•	7
7	Bootlegger	5,200	Jun-Aug		10		•		•				•	7
8	Banjo Bill	5,000	Jun-Aug		8	•	•					•	•	7
9	Manzanita	4,800	Jun-Aug		19	•	•		•			•	•	7
10	Beaver Creek	3,800	Apr-Sep	•	13	•	•		•				•	7
11	Clear Creek	3,200	Apr-Oct	•	18	•							•	7

1 Potato Patch

Location: About 14 miles southwest of Cottonwood, on Woodchute Mountain.
Sites: 35 tent and RV up to 22 feet. No hookups.
Road conditions: Paved.
Management: Prescott National Forest, 520-527-1119.
Finding the campground: From Cottonwood, drive about 14 miles south on Arizona Highway 89A to the pass on Mingus Mountain, then turn right into the campground.

Description: Located in a pine forest on the southeast corner of Woodchute Mountain, this campground is a good base for exploring the trails in the Woodchute Wilderness. Nearby Jerome was once a busy copper mining town and is now an artist's colony and popular tourist destination. You can learn about the history of the area at Jerome State Park, located in a former mansion. The nearest services are in Jerome; full services are in Cottonwood.

2 Mingus Mountain

Location: About 17 miles southwest of Cottonwood, on Mingus Mountain.
Sites: 24 tent and RV up to 22 feet. No hookups.
Road conditions: Paved, dirt.
Management: Prescott National Forest, 520-567-4121.
Finding the campground: From Cottonwood, drive about 14 miles south on Arizona Highway 89A to the pass on Mingus Mountain, then turn left (south) on Forest Road 104 and go about 3 miles to the campground.

Description: The campground is in the beautiful ponderosa pine forest on the summit plateau of Mingus Mountain. There are spectacular views of central Arizona from the nearby rim, and a network of hiking trails leading off the rim. Group camping is available. The nearest services are in Jerome; full services are in Prescott and Cottonwood.

3 Powell Springs

Location: About 19 miles east of Camp Verde, in the Black Hills.
Sites: 10 tent and RV up to 16 feet. No hookups.
Road conditions: Paved, all-weather dirt.
Management: Prescott National Forest, 520-567-4121.
Finding the campground: From Camp Verde on Interstate 17, drive about 7 miles south on I-17, then turn right (east) on Arizona Highway 169. Continue 7 miles, then turn right (north) on Cherry Road, Forest Road 75. Go about 5 miles to the campground.

Description: This small, out-of-the-way campground is tucked into the rugged Black Hills south of Mingus Mountain. You can use this campground as a base for mountain biking and exploring the Black Hills. The Pine Mountain and Cedar Mesa Wildernesses, southeast along the Verde Rim, have trails for backcountry hikers. The nearest services are in Dewey, 15 miles west, and Camp Verde, 19 miles northeast.

4 Dead Horse Ranch

Location: Cottonwood, in the Verde Valley.
Sites: 81 tent and RV. Water and electric hookups.
Road conditions: Paved.
Management: Dead Horse State Park, 520-634-5283.
Finding the campground: From Cottonwood, take 10th Street less than a mile to the park.

Description: The park features a nature trail and fishing. Showers and partial hookups are available. Group camping is available by reservation. Full services are available in Cottonwood. Nearby attractions include the historic mining town of Jerome, and Tuzigoot National Monument.

A cool mountain stream flows down the West Fork of Oak Creek.

5 Pine Flat

Location: About 12 miles north of Sedona, in Oak Creek Canyon.
Sites: 58 tent and RV up to 32 feet. No hookups.
Road conditions: Paved.
Management: Coconino National Forest, 520-282-4119.
Finding the campground: From Sedona, drive 12 miles north on Arizona Highway 89A. The campground is on both sides of the highway.

Description: The campground is in the cool depths of Oak Creek Canyon in a shady stand of ponderosa pines. Oak Creek borders the western edge of the campground; it is fished for trout. A trail climbs to the east rim of the canyon for spectacular views of the upper canyon. All Oak Creek campgrounds fill early on weekends and holidays. There are limited services in Oak Creek Canyon; the nearest full services are in Sedona.

6 Cave Spring

Location: About 10 miles north of Sedona, in Oak Creek Canyon.
Sites: 78 tent and RV up to 32 feet. No hookups.
Road conditions: Paved.
Management: Coconino National Forest, 520-282-4119.
Finding the campground: From Sedona, drive 10 miles north on Arizona Highway 89A, then turn left into the campground.

Description: The largest campground in Oak Creek Canyon, it is also located further from the highway than the others, which means you'll hear more of the creek and less of the traffic. It makes a fine base for exploring Oak Creek and its attractions, such as trout fishing and hiking. The canyon floor is forested with ponderosa pine. Deciduous trees, such as Arizona sycamore and Fremont cottonwood, surround Oak Creek, which flows past the eastern edge of the campground. These trees, along with others, create a fine display of fall color in October. Like all Oak Creek campgrounds, Cave Spring fills early on weekends and holidays. There are limited services in Oak Creek Canyon; the nearest full services are in Sedona.

7 Bootlegger

Location: About 8 miles north of Sedona, in Oak Creek Canyon.
Sites: 10 tent.
Road conditions: Paved.
Management: Coconino National Forest, 520-282-4119.
Finding the campground: From Sedona, drive 8 miles north on Arizona Highway 89A, then turn left into the campground.

Description: This small campground is squeezed between the highway and Oak Creek, in a stand of pine and oak. It features fishing in Oak Creek and hiking on several nearby trails. The historic AB Young Trail, built by an early settler, starts from the west side of the creek and climbs to the west rim of the canyon. Birdwatching is also popular along the permanent waters of the creek. Like all Oak Creek campgrounds, Bootlegger fills early on weekends and holidays. There are limited services in Oak Creek Canyon; the nearest full services are in Sedona.

8 Banjo Bill

Location: About 7 miles north of Sedona, in Oak Creek Canyon.
Sites: 8 tent.
Road conditions: Paved.
Management: Coconino National Forest, 520-282-4119.
Finding the campground: From Sedona, drive 7 miles north on Arizona Highway 89A, then turn sharply left into the campground.

Description: This is another small campground squeezed into the space between Oak Creek and the highway. As with the other popular Oak Creek campgrounds, it fills early on weekends and holidays. There are limited services in Oak Creek Canyon; the nearest full services are in Sedona.

9 Manzanita

Location: About 6 miles north of Sedona, in Oak Creek Canyon.
Sites: 19 tent.
Road conditions: Paved.
Management: Coconino National Forest, 520-282-4119.
Finding the campground: From Sedona, drive 6 miles north on Arizona Highway 89A, then turn right into the campground.

Description: This is the closest campground to Sedona. Like all Oak Creek campgrounds, Manzanita fills early on weekends and holidays. Trout fishing is popular in the creek, and there are several hiking trails nearby. The North Wilson Trail is an ambitious hike to the top of Wilson Mountain, and the Sterling Pass Trail follows an old Indian route to Sterling Canyon. There are limited services in Oak Creek Canyon; the nearest full services are in Sedona.

10 Beaver Creek

Location: About 17 miles southeast of Sedona, on Wet Beaver Creek.
Sites: 13 tent and RV up to 22 feet. No hookups.
Road conditions: Paved.
Management: Coconino National Forest, 520-567-4501.
Finding the campground: From Sedona, go 14 miles south on Arizona Highway 179, cross under Interstate 17, and continue 2.5 miles on Forest Road 618 to the campground. From I-17, take the Sedona exit. Turn east onto Forest Road 618.

Red rock formations create the skyline near Sedona.

Description: This small campground is near an interstate but still feels out of the way. It is located on the banks of Wet Beaver Creek, a permanent stream flowing from beneath the Mogollon Rim. The streamside riparian forest of Arizona sycamores and Fremont cottonwoods provides shade. Hiking is available on the nearby Apache Maid Trail, which follows the creek upstream, and along West Clear Creek, which is further south on FR 618. Other nearby attractions include Montezuma Well and Montezuma Castle National Monuments, which preserve unique ruins left by the people who lived in the area 1,000 years ago. The nearest services are in Camp Verde; full services are available in Sedona.

11 Clear Creek

Location: About 3 miles southeast of Camp Verde, on West Clear Creek.
Sites: 18 tent and RV up to 32 feet. No hookups.
Road conditions: Paved, all-weather dirt.
Management: Coconino National Forest, 520-567-4501.
Finding the campground: From Camp Verde, drive 8 miles east on Arizona Highway 260 to the campground, which is on the left.

Description: The campground is on West Clear Creek, a cold, permanent creek flowing from a deep canyon in the Mogollon Rim. The creek is popular with anglers and wildlife watchers. Though the campground is in desert grassland, shade is provided by the streamside trees. Group camping is available. Nearby attractions include Montezuma Well and Montezuma Castle National Monuments, and Fort Verde State Park. The nearest services are in Camp Verde; full services are available in Cottonwood, 20 miles west, and in Sedona, 26 miles north.

Valley of the Sun

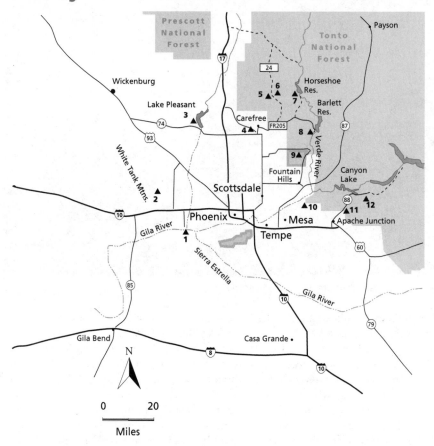

Phoenix and its sister cities in the Valley of the Sun are home to more than two million people, more than half the state's population. With such an urban concentration, it is hard to believe there are public campgrounds within easy reach. However, the desert valley lies on the edge of the rugged central mountains, and is bordered on the north and east by the 2.9 million acres of the Tonto National Forest, one of the largest in the country. In addition, several regional county parks have campgrounds. You can ride a bike or hike on trails in most of the regional parks, and there are miles of back roads and trails open to mountain bikers in the national forest. Backcountry hikers can find complete solitude in the Pine Mountain and Superstition Wildernesses. Boaters, water sports enthusiasts, and anglers flock to the many lakes impounded on the Verde and Salt Rivers northeast of the valley.

The valley is home to far too many events, museums, and other cultural activities to detail, but here are a few highlights. The Arizona Science Center offers hands-on science exhibits that appeal to kids. Adults should check out the Arizona Museum of History. If you are an art lover, do not miss the Phoenix Art Museum, and for Native American arts and crafts, visit the Heard Museum.

Children ages 4 to 12 will enjoy a wonderful hands-on art experience at the Arizona Museum for Youth in Mesa. If you are into airplanes, the Champlin Fighter Museum, also in Mesa, has a fine collection of authentic planes from World Wars I and II. In Coolidge, check out Casa Grande Ruins National Monument, which preserves a striking example of prehistoric Hohokam Native American architecture. The Hohokam people lived in the Valley of the Sun for hundreds of years, and built a thriving community based on farming by diverting the water of the Salt River through a valley-wide system of canals. In Phoenix, Pueblo Grande Museum and Cultural Park exhibits some of the Hohokam artifacts. Another place to learn about the valley's history is the Pioneer Living History Museum north of Phoenix. The Desert Botanical Garden is a great place to learn more about desert natural history.

For more information:
Phoenix & Valley of the Sun Convention & Visitors Bureau
400 E. Van Buren, Ste. 600
Phoenix, AZ 85004
602-254-6500
Fax: 602-253-4415

PHOENIX

		Elevation	Season	RV/Trailer	Sites	Drinking Water	Fishing	RV dump	Hiking trails	Boating	Boat launch	Handicap access	Fee ($)	Stay limit (days)
1	Estrella Mountain Regional Park	1,000	All year	•	•	•			•				•	14
2	White Tank Mountains Regional Park	1,400	All year	•	77	•			•			•	•	14
3	Lake Pleasant Regional Park	1,800	All year	•	148	•	•			•	•	•	•	14
4	Cave Creek Recreation Area	1,900	All year	•	38	•		•	•			•	•	14
5	Seven Springs	3,300	All year		23				•					14
6	CCC	3,300	All year	•	8				•					14
7	Horseshoe	1,900	All year	•	12		•			•	•		•	14
8	Riverside	1,600	All year		12		•			•			•	14
9	McDowell Mountain Regional Park	2,000	All year	•	76	•		•	•				•	14
10	Usery Mountain Recreation Area	2,000	All year	•	73	•			•				•	14
11	Lost Dutchman State Park	1,800	All year	•	35	•		•	•				•	14
12	Tortilla	1,800	Oct-Apr	•	77	•		•					•	14

1 Estrella Mountain Regional Park

Location: About 23 miles southwest of Phoenix, in the foothills of the Estrella Mountains.
Sites: "Unlimited" tent, 6 RV with full hookups, no size limit.
Road conditions: Paved.

The Superstition Mountains are home to varied odd rock formations.

Management: Maricopa County Parks and Recreation Department, 602-932-3811.

Finding the campground: From downtown Phoenix, go about 16 miles west on Interstate 10, then turn left at Exit 126 onto Estrella Parkway. Follow the signs 7 miles to the park and campground.

Description: The park and campground are located at the north end of the rugged Sierra Estrella Mountains. There are 35 miles of trails, a golf course, and a rodeo arena. Group camping is available. Some partial hookups are available, as are showers. The nearest full services are in Phoenix.

2 White Tank Mountains Regional Park

Location: About 33 miles west of Phoenix, in the foothills of the White Tank Mountains.

Sites: 40 tent, 37 RV with no size limit. No hookups.

Road conditions: Paved.

Management: Maricopa County Parks and Recreation Department, 602-935-2505.

Finding the campground: From Phoenix, go about 18 miles west on Interstate 10, exit at Cotton Lane, Exit 124, then go north 7 miles. Turn left on Olive Avenue, and continue about 8 miles, past the park entrance, to the campground near the end of White Tanks Mountain Drive.

Description: The park and campground are located in the eastern foothills of the White Tank Mountains, in the Sonoran desert. There are 29 miles of trails for hikers, horses, and mountain bikers. A group camp area and a playground are available, as are showers. The nearest services are in Phoenix.

3 Lake Pleasant Regional Park

Location: About 36 miles northwest of Phoenix, at Lake Pleasant.

Sites: 148 RV, no size limit. Some full hookups.

Road conditions: Paved.

Management: Maricopa County Parks and Recreation Department, 602-780-9875.

Finding the campground: From downtown Phoenix, go about 24 miles north on Interstate 17, then exit at Arizona Highway 74. Go left (west) 5 miles, then turn right (north) to remain on Arizona Highway 74, and drive 6 miles to the park entrance signs.

Description: This is a desert campground, so it will be hot in the summer. Full hookups are available at all sites. Showers are available. Fishing, boating, water-skiing, sailboarding, and other water sports are popular on Lake Pleasant. Boat rentals are available. The campground can be used as a base for exploring the rugged Hieroglyphic Mountains to the northwest. The nearest full services are in Phoenix.

4 Cave Creek Recreation Area

Location: About 33 miles north of Phoenix, in the foothills of the New River Mountains.
Sites: 38 RV, no size limit. Some full hookups.
Road conditions: Paved.
Management: Maricopa County Parks and Recreation Department, 602-465-0431.
Finding the campground: From downtown Phoenix, drive about 24 miles north on Interstate 17, then exit at Arizona Highway 74. Go 6 miles east to 32nd Street, then turn left and go 3 miles to the recreation area entrance.

Description: The recreation area and campground are in the Sonoran desert foothills near Cave Creek. It features both hiking and horse trails; horse rentals are available. Mountain biking is also popular in the area. Partial hookups are available, as are showers. The nearest services are in Cave Creek; the nearest full services are in Phoenix.

5 Seven Springs

Location: 18 miles north of Carefree, in the New River Mountains.
Sites: 23 tent.
Road conditions: Dirt.
Management: Tonto National Forest, 602-595-3300.
Finding the campground: From Carefree, drive 18 miles north on Cave Creek Road, which becomes Forest Road 24.

Description: This campground is just south of CCC Campground (described below). Although it is open all year, summers are very hot. The nearest full services are in Carefree. The Cave Creek Trailhead is just north of CCC Campground.

6 CCC

Location: 19 miles north of Carefree, in the New River Mountains.
Sites: 8 tent and RV up to 16 feet. No hookups.
Road conditions: Dirt.
Management: Tonto National Forest, 602-595-3300.
Finding the campground: From Carefree, drive 19 miles north on Cave Creek Road, which becomes Forest Road 24.

Description: Located in the Sonoran desert country north of Phoenix, this campground is best in the fall, winter, and spring, though it is open all year. Group camping, by reservation only, is available at nearby Cave Creek Group Campground. The campground can be used as a base for exploring the New River Mountains and adjoining areas of the Tonto National Forest by vehicle or mountain bike. The Cave Creek Trailhead is just north of this campground. The nearest services are in Carefree, and the nearest full services are in Phoenix.

Weavers Needle is the most famous landmark in the Superstition Mountains.

7 Horseshoe

Location: 21 miles northeast of Carefree, on the Verde River.
Sites: 12 tent and RV up to 22 feet. No hookups.
Road conditions: Paved, dirt.
Management: Tonto National Forest, 602-595-3300.
Finding the campground: From Carefree, go 5 miles east on Cave Creek Road, then turn right on Bartlett Dam Road (FR 205). After 6 miles, turn left on Horseshoe Dam Road, then continue 10 miles.

Description: This Sonoran desert campground is on the Verde River below Horseshoe Dam. Fishing and boating are popular on the river. The nearest services are in Carefree, and the nearest full services are in Phoenix.

8 Riverside

Location: About 23 miles east of Carefree, on the Verde River.
Sites: 12 tent.
Road conditions: Paved, dirt.
Management: Tonto National Forest, 602-595-3300.
Finding the campground: From Carefree, go 5 miles east on Cave Creek Road, then turn right on Bartlett Dam Road (FR 205). Drive 16 miles, turn right, and go 3 miles to the campground.

Description: Located in the Sonoran desert below Bartlett Dam, this campground is a popular access point on the Verde River. Boating, rafting, and fishing are popular activities on the river. The nearest services are in Carefree, and the nearest full services are in Phoenix.

9 McDowell Mountain Regional Park

Location: About 22 miles east of Scottsdale.
Sites: 76 tent and RV. Water and electric hookups.
Road conditions: Paved.
Management: Maricopa County Parks and Recreation Department, 602-471-0173.
Finding the campground: From Scottsdale, go 13 miles east on Shea Boulevard, then turn left on Fountain Hills Boulevard, which becomes McDowell Mountain Road. Turn left at the park entrance, and follow the signs to the family campground.

Description: The park is located in the northeast foothills of the McDowell Mountains. The features include hiking, riding, and mountain bike trails. Group camping is available by reservation. Limited services are available in Fountain Hills, and full services in Scottsdale.

10 Usery Mountain Recreation Area

Location: About 12 miles northeast of Mesa.
Sites: 73 tent and RV. No hookups.
Road conditions: Paved.
Management: Maricopa County Parks and Recreation Department, 602-984-0032.
Finding the campground: From Mesa, drive about 12 miles north on Ellsworth Road, which becomes Usery Pass Road. Turn right onto the park entrance road, and follow the signs to the family campground.

Description: This desert campground is located in the Usery Mountains, and features an extensive system of hiking, riding, and mountain biking trails. Group camping is available by reservation. Full services are available in Mesa.

11 Lost Dutchman State Park

Location: About 5 miles northeast of Apache Junction, in the foothills of the Superstition Mountains.
Sites: 35 tent and RV. No hookups.
Road conditions: Paved.
Management: Lost Dutchman State Park, 602-982-4455.
Finding the campground: From Apache Junction, go north 5 miles on Arizona Highway 88.

Description: This park's dramatic setting in the Sonoran desert at the base of the Superstition Mountains is a good jumping-off point for exploration of the area. The park features nature trails, and the nearby Superstition Wilderness has many miles of backcountry trails. Full services are available in Apache Junction.

12 Tortilla

Location: About 18 miles northeast of Apache Junction, in the Superstition Mountains.
Sites: 77 tent and RV up to 22 feet. No hookups.
Road conditions: Paved.
Management: Tonto National Forest, 602-379-6446.
Finding the campground: From Apache Junction, go 18 miles northeast on Arizona Highway 88, past Canyon Lake.

Description: Surrounded by the famous Superstition Mountains, this campground makes a good base to explore the historic Apache Trail (Arizona Highway 88) and the surrounding area. The Superstition Wilderness, to the south, features a network of backcountry trails. A post office, restaurant, and gift shop are located at Tortilla Flat Resort across the road from the campground. It is 2 miles west to Canyon Lake, which has cold and warm water fisheries, and a full service marina with boat rentals, restaurant, and lake tours. The nearest full services are in Apache Junction. This campground is closed during the summer.

High Country

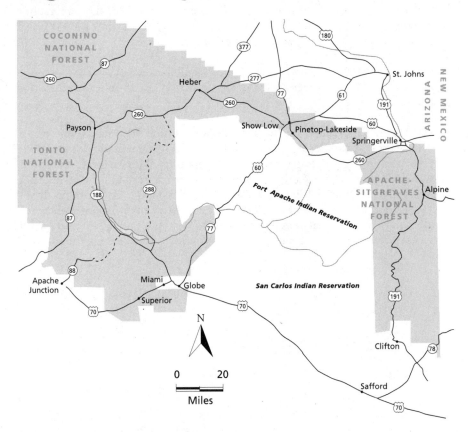

Arizona's High Country is a camping and outdoor recreation paradise. It is somewhat misnamed, because it includes elevations ranging from 2,000 feet in the Sonoran desert country in the Tonto Basin to the 11,000-foot White Mountains. The High Country contains the ruggedly beautiful country south of the Mogollon Rim around Payson, including the central Mogollon Rim around Show Low, and encompasses the fir and spruce forests of the White Mountains around Alpine. Two national forests, the Tonto and the Apache-Sitgreaves, cover much of the area. The White Mountain and San Carlos Apache Tribes manage a large area south of the central Mogollon Rim. Dozens of mountain lakes provide diverse fishing, boating, paddling, and other water sports. The spectacular Salt River Canyon is one of the premier white water rivers in the state.

PAYSON

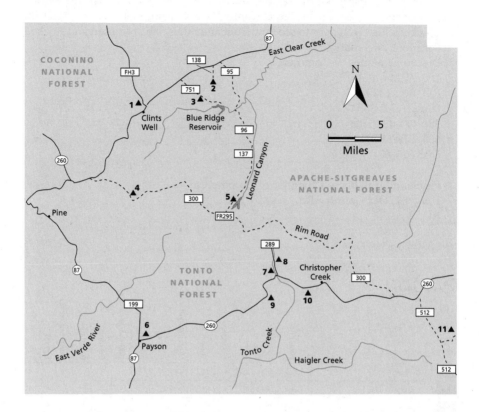

Payson is in the center of the mountain country made famous by western writer Zane Grey, who often wrote from a small cabin close under the 2,000-foot escarpment of the Mogollon Rim. Just an hour-and-a-half drive from Phoenix, the Payson area is a popular summer retreat. The Mazatzal Wilderness, one of the largest in the state, bounds the area on the west. Containing the northern half of the Mazatzal Mountains, this craggy range has miles of hiking trails for the back-country walker. The smaller Hellsgate Wilderness contains Tonto and Haigler Creeks, which form deep, rugged canyons. Miles of forest roads and trails are open to mountain bikers. Probably the best known trail is the Highline National Recreation Trail, which winds under the Mogollon Rim for miles. And yes, there are campgrounds! In addition to the standard Forest Service campgrounds listed here, the Tonto National Forest has a number of small, primitive campsites scattered through the forest. And, you can camp dispersed nearly anywhere in the forest.

In Payson, check out the Zane Grey and Rim Country Museums to learn more about the history of the region. North of Payson, you can visit the world's largest travertine natural bridge at Tonto Natural Bridge State Park. Visit the Tonto Creek Fish Hatchery to see how trout and other fish are raised and stocked.

For more information:
Payson Chamber of Commerce
100 W. Main St.
P.O. Box 1380
Payson, AZ 85547
520-474-4515
800-6-PAYSON
Fax: 520-474-8812

Pine and Strawberry Chamber of Commerce
Hwy. 87, Old Country Rd.
P.O. Box 196
Pine, AZ 85544
520-476-3547

PAYSON

		Elevation	Season	RV/Trailer	Sites	Drinking Water	Fishing	RV dump	Hiking trails	Boating	Boat launch	Handicap access	Fee ($)	Stay limit (days)
1	Clints Well	7,000	May-Nov	•	12									14
2	Blue Ridge	7,300	May-Sep	•	10	•			•				•	14
3	Rock Crossing	7,500	May-Sep	•	35	•	•			•			•	14
4	Kehl Springs	7,500	All year	•	8									14
5	Knoll Lake	7,400	May-Sep	•	33	•	•			•	•		•	14
6	Houston Mesa	5,100	All year	•	75	•		•	•			•	•	14
7	Lower Tonto Creek	5,600	Apr-Oct	•	17	•	•		•				•	14
8	Upper Tonto Creek	5,600	Apr-Oct	•	9	•	•						•	14
9	Ponderosa	5,600	All year	•	61	•		•	•				•	14
10	Christopher Creek	5,800	Apr-Oct	•	43	•	•					•	•	14
11	Valentine Ridge	6,700	Apr-Nov	•	9									14

1 Clints Well

Location: About 45 miles north of Payson, on the Mogollon Plateau.
Sites: 12 tent and RV up to 22 feet. No hookups.
Road conditions: Paved.
Management: Coconino National Forest, 520-354-2216.

Finding the campground: From Payson, drive about 45 miles north on Arizona Highway 87. Turn left on Forest Highway 3, go 0.5 mile, then turn left into the campground.

Description: Located in tall, old-growth ponderosa pines, Clints Well Campground is a convenient base for exploring the Mogollon Rim country, easily accessible from numerous forest roads leading off FR 3 and AZ 87. Unlimited mountain biking is possible on the forest road system, many of which are winding, unimproved tracks. There are several hiking areas in the vicinity, including the historic Cabin Loop trail system, the Arizona Trail, and the West Clear Creek Wilderness. Trails also lead into East Clear Creek. Limited services are available at Clints Well; the nearest full services are in Payson and Winslow.

2 Blue Ridge

Location: About 50 miles north of Payson, on the Mogollon Plateau.
Sites: 10 tent and RV up to 22 feet. No hookups.
Road conditions: All-weather dirt.
Management: Coconino National Forest, 520-477-2255.
Finding the campground: From Payson, drive about 53 miles north on Arizona Highway 87, then turn right on Forest Road 138 and go 1 mile.

Description: This small campground is located in a stately pine forest. It is a good base for exploration of the Mogollon Plateau and its canyons and streams. The Arizona Trail passes through here on its way from Utah to Mexico, and there are other hiking trails in the area. Miles of forest roads provide good mountain biking. Fishing and boating are popular on Blue Ridge Reservoir, a small lake in a deep canyon. See Rock Crossing Campground below for information. Limited services are available in Clints Well. The nearest full services are in Winslow.

3 Rock Crossing

Location: About 53 miles north of Payson, near Blue Ridge Reservoir.
Sites: 35 tent and RV up to 22 feet. No hookups.
Road conditions: All-weather dirt.
Management: Coconino National Forest, 520-477-2255.
Finding the campground: From Payson, drive about 50 miles north on Arizona Highway 87, then turn right on Forest Road 751 and go 3 miles to the campground on the right.

Description: Located in the pine forest near Blue Ridge Reservoir, the campground is named for a nearby crossing of East Clear Creek. Many canyons cut through the Mogollon Plateau, and crossing points are limited. In the early ranching days, the few good crossings were quickly named. Rock Crossing is usually submerged under Blue Ridge Reservoir, but other historic crossings are still in use. The reservoir is 3 miles east out on FR 751, and is a popular fishing lake. It is also a good lake for paddlers—the narrow canyons are the next best thing to a

Tonto Creek wanders through the rugged country below the Mogollon Rim.

river trip. Limited services are available in Clints Well; the nearest full services are in Winslow and Payson.

4 Kehl Springs

Location: About 40 miles north of Payson, on the Mogollon Rim.
Sites: 8 tent and RV up to 22 feet. No hookups.
Road conditions: Dirt.
Management: Coconino National Forest, 520-354-2216.
Finding the campground: From Payson, drive about 34 miles north on Arizona Highway 87, then turn right on Forest Road 300. Go 6 miles to the campground.

Description: This small campground is near the edge of the Mogollon Rim in a stand of shady ponderosa pines. It's also on the Rim Road, a scenic drive along the top of the Mogollon Rim, and near the historic Crook Trail. During the Apache Wars, General Crook built a military wagon road along the rim to connect a number of U.S. Army forts. The approximate route of the wagon road is followed by FR 300; the exact route has been marked by the Forest Service. Hiking and mountain biking is virtually unlimited on the many trails and roads on the plateau north of the rim. Limited services are available at Clints Well; the nearest full services are in Payson.

5 Knoll Lake

Location: About 52 miles northeast of Payson, on the Mogollon Rim.
Sites: 33 tent and RV up to 22 feet. No hookups.
Road conditions: Dirt.
Management: Coconino National Forest, 520-477-2255.
Finding the campground: From Payson, drive 28 miles east on Arizona Highway 260, then turn left on Forest Road 300. Go 20 miles, turn right on Forest Road 295E, and go 4 miles to the campground.

Description: The campground and lake are several miles north of the Mogollon Rim in ponderosa pine forest. Fishing and boating are popular on this small but scenic lake. The surrounding Rim Country offers many opportunities for mountain biking, hiking, and exploring. The nearest full services are in Payson.

6 Houston Mesa

Location: North side of Payson.
Sites: 75 tent and RV up to 30 feet. No hookups.
Road conditions: Paved.
Management: Tonto National Forest, 520-474-7900.
Finding the campground: From Payson, drive to the north end of town on Arizona Highway 87, then turn right on Forest Road 199.

Description: This new campground is conveniently located just north of Payson. It is a great starting point for exploring the Payson area and the Rim Country. It has a nature trail. The nearest full services are in Payson.

7 | Lower Tonto Creek

Location: About 15 miles northeast of Payson, on Tonto Creek.
Sites: 17 tent and RV up to 22 feet. No hookups.
Road conditions: All-weather dirt.
Management: Tonto National Forest, 520-474-7900.
Finding the campground: From Payson, drive 15 miles northeast on Arizona Highway 260, then turn left on Forest Road 289.

Description: Located near the headwaters of Tonto Creek under the Mogollon Rim, this campground is a good base for exploration of this historic section of the state. The Highline National Recreation Trail is several miles north, under the Mogollon Rim. There are more trails in the Hellsgate Wilderness, located south of AZ 260. Fishing is popular in the creek. Limited services are available at Christopher Creek. The nearest full services are in Payson.

8 | Upper Tonto Creek

Location: About 16 miles northeast of Payson, on Tonto Creek.
Sites: 9 tent and RV up to 22 feet. No hookups.
Road conditions: Paved.
Management: Tonto National Forest, 520-474-7900.
Finding the campground: From Payson, drive 15 miles northeast on Arizona Highway 260, then turn left on Forest Road 289. Continue about 1 mile to the campground.

Description: The campground is on Tonto Creek below the Mogollon Rim. There are many hiking trails in the area, including the Highline National Recreation Trail. Fishing is popular in the creek. Limited services are available at Christopher Creek. The nearest full services are in Payson.

9 | Ponderosa

Location: About 12 miles northeast of Payson, below the Mogollon Rim..
Sites: 61 tent and RV up to 60 feet. No hookups.
Road conditions: Paved.
Management: Tonto National Forest, 520-474-7900.
Finding the campground: From Payson, drive 12 miles northeast on Arizona Highway 260, then turn right into the campground.

Description: The campground features a self-guided nature trail. Additional hikes include trails into the nearby Hellsgate Wilderness, the Highline National Recreation Trail, and side trails. Group camping is available. Some services are available in Christopher Creek; the nearest full services are in Payson.

10 Christopher Creek

Location: About 19 miles northeast of Payson, on Christopher Creek.
Sites: 43 tent and RV up to 22 feet. No hookups.
Road conditions: Paved.
Management: Tonto National Forest, 520-474-7900.
Finding the campground: From Payson, drive 19 miles northeast on Arizona Highway 260, then turn right into the campground.

Description: Fishing is popular in Christopher Creek, a cold trout stream that issues from below the Mogollon Rim. Limited services are available in Christopher Creek; the nearest full services are in Payson.

11 Valentine Ridge

Location: About 41 miles east of Payson, below the Mogollon Rim.
Sites: 9 tent and RV up to 16 feet. No hookups.
Road conditions: Dirt.
Management: Tonto National Forest, 520-462-4300.
Finding the campground: From Payson, go 33 miles east on Arizona Highway 260, then turn right onto Forest Road 512. Continue 6 miles, then turn left onto Forest Road 188 and go 2 miles to the campground.

Description: This is a small campground in an isolated setting below the Mogollon Rim. It is a good base for exploring the central Mogollon Rim country, and the Sierra Ancha Mountains to the south. A 4-mile mountain bike trail starts in the campground. Limited services are available in Christopher Creek; full services are in Payson.

GLOBE

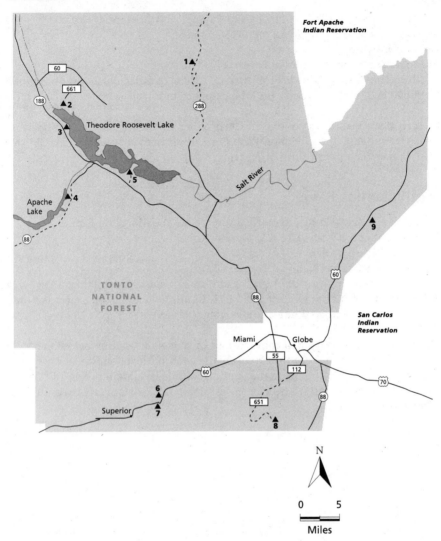

North and west of the small city of Globe is an incredible variety of country, ranging from Sonoran desert to pine-forested mountains. The Four Peaks, Superstition, Sierra Ancha, Salome, and Salt River Canyon Wildernesses provide backcountry opportunities for hikers and river runners. Miles of forest roads and trails outside the wildernesses offer some great mountain biking. Several large lakes on the Salt River are very popular with boaters and anglers. The largest of these, Theodore Roosevelt Lake, was the first federal reclamation project in the West. The original masonry dam was built from local stone quarried at the site.

Tonto National Monument, near Theodore Roosevelt Lake, preserves a fine example of a cliff dwelling from the Salado people, who occupied the area during the 13th through the 15th centuries. The monument was proclaimed by Theodore

Roosevelt, who used the newly authorized Antiquities Act to create the nation's first national monuments and national wildlife refuges. Just outside the town of Superior, you'll find Boyce Thompson Arboretum, a popular birding destination with a variety of habitats. The wildflower displays are exquisite here, and the Arboretum provides a special picnic area.

For more information:
Globe-Miami Chamber of Commerce
P.O. Box 2539
1360 N. Broad St.
Globe, AZ 85501
520-425-4495
800-804-5623
Fax: 520-425-3410

Superior Chamber of Commerce
151 Main St.
Superior, AZ 85273
520-689-2441

GLOBE

		Elevation	Season	RV/Trailer	Sites	Drinking Water	Fishing	RV dump	Hiking trails	Boating	Boat launch	Handicap access	Fee ($)	Stay limit (days)
1	Rose Creek	5,400	Apr-Nov	•	5	•								14
2	Indian Point	2,200	All year	•	90		•			•	•	•	•	14
3	Cholla	2,200	All year	•	200	•	•	•	•	•	•	•	•	14
4	Burnt Corral	1,900	All year	•	79	•	•			•	•		•	14
5	Windy Hill	2,200	All year	•	346	•	•	•	•	•	•	•	•	14
6	Devils Canyon	4,000	All year		5									1
7	Oak Flat	4,200	All year	•	16									14
8	Pinal	7,500	May-Nov	•	19	•								14
9	Jones Water	4,500	All year	•	12									14

1 Rose Creek

Location: About 41 miles north of Globe, in the Sierra Ancha Mountains.
Sites: 5 tent and RV up to 16 feet. No hookups.
Road conditions: Paved, all-weather dirt.
Management: Tonto National Forest, 520-462-4300.
Finding the campground: From Globe, go about 4 miles west on U.S. Highway 60, then turn right on Arizona Highway 88. Continue 13 miles, then turn right on Arizona Highway 288. Continue 24 miles, then turn left on Forest Road 152 and go 0.25 mile to the campground.

Four Peaks is a striking summit visible from many places in the High Country west and north of Globe.

Description: This small, remote campground is a fine base for exploring the nearby Sierra Ancha and Salome Wildernesses, which have a number of hiking trails. The nearest services are in Young; the nearest full services are in Globe.

2 Indian Point

Location: About 46 miles northwest of Globe, on Theodore Roosevelt Lake.
Sites: 90 tent and RV up to 16 feet. No hookups.
Road conditions: Paved, dirt.
Management: Tonto National Forest, 520-467-3200.
Finding the campground: From Globe, drive about 4 miles west on U.S. Highway 60, then turn right on Arizona Highway 88. Continue 28 miles to Roosevelt Dam, then continue across Roosevelt Lake Bridge on AZ 188. Go another 10 miles, then turn right on Forest Road 60, go 2 miles, then turn right on FR 661 and continue 2 miles to the campground.

Description: This new campground is on the northwest end of Theodore Roosevelt Lake It's a low-elevation, desert campground, popular with anglers, boaters, and water sports enthusiasts. The nearest services are in Roosevelt; the nearest full services are in Payson and Globe.

3 Cholla

Location: About 38 miles northwest of Globe, on Theodore Roosevelt Lake.
Sites: 200 tent and RV up to 32 feet. No hookups.
Road conditions: Paved.

Management: Tonto National Forest, 520-467-3200.

Finding the campground: From Globe, drive about 4 miles west on U.S. Highway 60, then turn right on Arizona Highway 88. Continue 28 miles to Roosevelt Dam, then continue across Roosevelt Lake Bridge on Arizona Highway 188. Go 6 miles to the campground, which is on the right.

Description: This is a desert campground on the shore of Theodore Roosevelt Lake. It is the largest completely solar-operated campground in the country. Open year-round, it is hot in summer. A public boat launch gives ready access to the huge reservoir for anglers, boaters, and water sports enthusiasts. Nearby Tonto National Monument preserves a fine set of Native American ruins. The nearest services are in Roosevelt, and the nearest full services are in Globe or Miami.

4 Burnt Corral

Location: About 38 miles northwest of Globe, on Apache Lake.

Sites: 79 tent and RV up to 22 feet. No hookups.

Road conditions: Paved, all-weather dirt.

Management: Tonto National Forest, 520-467-3200.

Finding the campground: From Globe, drive about 4 miles west on U.S. Highway 60, then turn right on Arizona Highway 88. Continue 28 miles to Roosevelt Dam, then turn left and continue 6 miles on AZ 88. Turn right on Forest Road 183 and go less than a mile to the campground.

Description: Located right on the shore of Apache Lake, this low-elevation, desert campground has a boat launch and is popular with anglers, boaters, and water sports enthusiasts. The nearest services are in Roosevelt; the nearest full services are in Globe.

5 Windy Hill

Location: About 30 miles northwest of Globe, on Theodore Roosevelt Lake.

Sites: 346 tent and RV up to 32 feet. No hookups.

Road conditions: Paved, dirt.

Management: Tonto National Forest, 520-467-3200.

Finding the campground: From Globe, drive about 4 miles west on U.S. Highway 60, then turn right on Arizona Highway 88. Continue 25 miles to Forest Road 82, then turn right and go about 1.5 miles to the campground.

Description: This is another desert campground on the shore of Theodore Roosevelt Lake. This is the largest Forest Service campground in the country. Though it is open year-round, it is hot in summer. There is a public boat launch. The campground is also a possible base for exploring the nearby Superstition Wilderness. The nearest services are in Roosevelt, and the nearest full services are in Globe or Miami.

6 | Devils Canyon

Location: About 16 miles southwest of Globe.
Sites: 5 tent.
Road conditions: Paved.
Management: Tonto National Forest, 520-402-6200.
Finding the campground: From Globe, drive about 16 miles west on U.S. Highway 60, then turn right into the campground. (This turnoff is about 6 miles east of Superior).

Description: This campground is set in a rugged oak and pinyon pine area near the headwaters of Devils Canyon, conveniently near the highway. Like Oak Flat Campground, it's a good base for exploring the nearby backcountry. Queen Creek Canyon, west along the highway, is a popular rock climbing area. Limited services are in Superior; full services are available in Globe.

7 | Oak Flat

Location: About 18 miles southwest of Globe.
Sites: 16 tent and RV up to 22 feet. No hookups.
Road conditions: Paved.
Management: Tonto National Forest, 520-402-6200.
Finding the campground: From Globe, drive about 18 miles west on U.S. Highway 60, then turn left into the campground. (This turnoff is about 4 miles east of Superior).

Description: This campground is pleasant all year because of its moderate elevation in an oak and pinyon pine–juniper flat. Its main attraction is the convenient location for the traveler. Devils Canyon and Apache Leap are nearby attractions for backcountry explorers. Limited services are in Superior; full services are available in Globe.

8 | Pinal

Location: 15 miles south of Globe, in the Pinal Mountains.
Sites: 19 tent and RV up to 16 feet. No hookups.
Road conditions: Paved, dirt.
Management: Tonto National Forest, 520-402-6200.
Finding the campground: From Globe, drive 3 miles south on Forest Road 112, then turn right on Forest Road 55. Continue 3 miles, then turn left on Forest Road 651. Go 9 miles to the campground.

Description: This pair of small campgrounds is located high on the pine and fir–forested slopes of Pinal Mountain, a popular mountain escape in the Globe area. A network of forest roads offers mountain bikers a chance to explore. Full services are available in Globe.

9 Jones Water

Location: 18 miles northeast of Globe.
Sites: 12 tent and RV up to 16 feet. No hookups.
Road conditions: Paved.
Management: Tonto National Forest, 520-425-7189.
Finding the campground: From Globe, drive 18 miles northeast on U.S. Highway 60; the campground is on the right.
Description: The main attraction of this small campground is its convenient location right along the highway, though the surrounding country would be interesting to explore. The nearest services are in Globe.

SHOW LOW

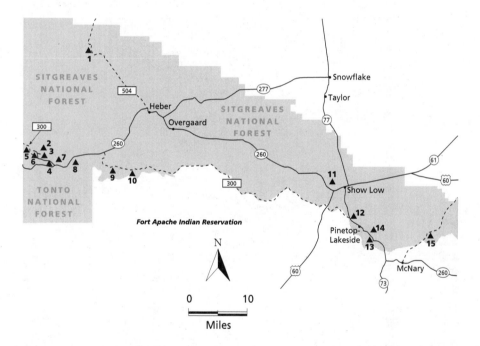

Show Low and its close neighbor, Pinetop-Lakeside, are located at the eastern end of the central Mogollon Rim in the Apache-Sitgreaves National Forest. Both towns have become very popular summer retreats for the desert dwellers of Phoenix and Tucson. The small town of Heber is near the western end. Stretching for miles, the Mogollon Plateau country just north of the Rim itself is a pine-forested plateau cut by numerous canyons that drain northward. Dozens of small, manmade lakes dot these canyons and provide both angling and boating. Many of the lakes are limited to small motors or electric motors, so they are enjoyable for canoeists and other paddlers. Many of the campgrounds in the area are located at or near the lakes. Mountain bikers can enjoy great cruises on miles of cool, shady forest roads.

North of Show Low, you can get an idea of what it was like to settle this country by touring some of the 100 pioneer homes preserved in the town of Snowflake. Visit the Fort Apache Historic Park near Whiteriver for a perspective on the history of Apache country. Fort Apache was an important post for the army troops led by General George Crook during the Apache wars of the last century. The Apache Cultural Center preserves the rich heritage of the Apache Tribe.

For more information:

Heber Chamber of Commerce
P.O. Box 550
Heber, AZ 85928
520-535-4406
Fax: 520-535-5762

Pinetop-Lakeside Chamber of
Commerce
592 W. White Mountain Blvd.
Lakeside, AZ 85929-3112
520-367-4290
Fax: 520-368-8528

Show Low Chamber of Commerce
951 W. Deuce of Clubs
P.O. Box 1083
Show Low, AZ 85901
520-537-2326
Fax: 520-537-2326

Snowflake-Taylor Chamber of
Commerce
P.O. Box 776
Snowflake, AZ 85937
520-536-4331

SHOW LOW

		Elevation	Season	RV/Trailer	Sites	Drinking Water	Fishing	RV dump	Hiking trails	Boating	Boat launch	Handicap access	Fee ($)	Stay limit (days)
1	Chevelon Crossing	6,500	Mar-Dec	•	6	•								14
2	Spillway	7,500	May-Sep	•	26	•	•	•	•	•	•		•	14
3	Crook	7,500	May-Sep	•	26	•	•	•	•				•	14
4	Aspen	7,500	May-Sep	•	136	•	•	•	•	•	•		•	14
5	Mogollon	7,500	May-Sep	•	26	•	•	•	•				•	14
6	Rim	7,500	May-Sep	•	26	•	•						•	14
7	Sink Hole	7,500	May-Sep	•	26	•	•						•	14
8	Canyon Point	7,600	May-Sep	•	117	•		•	•				•	14
9	Black Canyon Rim	7,600	May-Oct	•	21	•	•						•	14
10	Gentry	7,700	May-Oct	•	6									14
11	Fool Hollow Lake Recreation Area	6,300	All year	•	125	•	•	•	•	•	•	•	•	14
12	Show Low Lake County Park	7,000	All year	•	75	•	•			•	•		•	14
13	Lakeside	7,000	May-Sep	•	83	•					•	•	•	14
14	Scott Reservoir	6,740	All year		10		•		•	•	•			14
15	Los Burros	7,900	May-Oct	•	10			•						14

1 Chevelon Crossing

Location: About 19 miles northwest of Heber, in Chevelon Canyon.
Sites: 6 tent and RV up to 16 feet. No hookups.
Road conditions: Paved, all-weather dirt.
Management: Apache-Sitgreaves National Forest, 520-289-2471.
Finding the campground: From Heber, drive 1 mile west on Arizona Highway 260, then turn right on Forest Road 504. Continue 18 miles to the campground.

Description: This small, remote campground is a good choice if you want to get away from crowds. It is also a good base for exploring Chevelon Canyon and the Mogollon Plateau country. Limited services are available in Heber, and the nearest full services are in Winslow.

2 Spillway

Location: About 26 miles west of Heber, near Woods Canyon Lake.
Sites: 26 tent and RV up to 16 feet. No hookups.
Road conditions: Paved.
Management: Apache-Sitgreaves National Forest, 520-289-2471.
Finding the campground: From Heber, drive 22 miles west on Arizona Highway 260, then turn right on Forest Road 300. Go 3 miles, then turn right on Forest Road 105. Bear right to reach the campground in about 1 mile.

Description: One of several campgrounds in the pines near Woods Canyon Lake, this campground is popular with anglers. It is also near the Mogollon Rim and the historic General Crook Trail, so it makes a good base for exploration. Easy accessibility from the highway means the campground will fill up early on summer weekends. A group campground is also available. Limited supplies are available nearby. Limited services are available in Heber, and the nearest full services are in Payson.

3 Crook

Location: About 25 miles west of Heber, near Woods Canyon Lake.
Sites: 26 tent and RV up to 16 feet. No hookups.
Road conditions: Paved.
Management: Apache-Sitgreaves National Forest, 520-289-2471.
Finding the campground: From Heber, drive 22 miles west on Arizona Highway 260, then turn right on Forest Road 300. Go 3 miles, then turn right on Forest Road 105.

Description: Another campground in the pines near Woods Canyon Lake, this campground is popular with anglers. Easy accessibility from the highway means the campground fills up early on summer weekends. Limited supplies are available nearby. Full services are available in Payson.

4 Aspen

Location: About 25 miles west of Heber, near Woods Canyon Lake.
Sites: 136 tent and RV up to 32 feet. No hookups.
Road conditions: Paved.
Management: Apache-Sitgreaves National Forest, 520-289-2471.
Finding the campground: From Heber, drive 22 miles west on Arizona Highway 260, then turn right on Forest Road 300. Go 3 miles, then turn right on Forest Road 105.

Description: This is the largest campground near Woods Canyon Lake. Easy accessibility from the highway means the campground fills up early on summer weekends. Limited supplies are available nearby. Full services are available in Payson.

5 Mogollon

Location: About 26 miles west of Heber, near Woods Canyon Lake.
Sites: 26 tent and RV up to 32 feet. No hookups.
Road conditions: Paved.
Management: Apache-Sitgreaves National Forest, 520-289-2471.
Finding the campground: From Heber, drive 22 miles west on Arizona Highway 260, then turn right on Forest Road 300. Go 4 miles to the campground, which is on the left.

Description: Another campground in the pines near Woods Canyon Lake, this campground is popular with anglers and boaters. Easy accessibility from the highway means the campground fills up early on summer weekends. Limited supplies are available nearby. Full services are available in Payson.

6 Rim

Location: About 23 miles west of Heber, near Willow Springs Lake.
Sites: 26 tent and RV up to 32 feet. No hookups.
Road conditions: Paved.
Management: Apache-Sitgreaves National Forest, 520-535-4481.
Finding the campground: From Heber, drive 22 miles west on Arizona Highway 260, then turn right on Forest Road 300. Go less than a mile to the campground, which is on the left.

Description: This campground is near Willow Springs Lake, so it is popular with anglers. It is also near the Mogollon Rim and several historic trails, including the General Crook Historic Trail. The nearest services are in Heber, and the nearest full services are in Payson.

7 Sink Hole

Location: About 21 miles southwest of Heber, near Willow Springs Lake.
Sites: 26 tent and RV up to 32 feet. No hookups.
Road conditions: Paved.
Management: Apache-Sitgreaves National Forest, 520-535-4481.
Finding the campground: From Heber, drive 21 miles west on Arizona Highway 260, then turn right on Forest Road 149.

Description: This campground is near Willow Springs Lake, so it is popular with anglers. It is also near the Mogollon Rim and several historic trails. The nearest services are in Heber, and the nearest full services are in Payson.

8 Canyon Point

Location: About 18 miles southwest of Heber, near the Mogollon Rim.
Sites: 117 tent and RV up to 32 feet. No hookups.
Road conditions: Paved.
Management: Apache-Sitgreaves National Forest, 520-535-4481.
Finding the campground: From Heber, drive 18 miles west on Arizona Highway 260, then turn left into the campground.

Description: This large campground is near the highway. Its location makes it a convenient base for exploring the Mogollon Rim country and the numerous canyons and historic trails in the area. Of course, the campground is handy for the traveler also. A group campsite is available, as are showers. The nearest services are in Heber, and the nearest full services are in Payson.

9 Black Canyon Rim

Location: About 15 miles southwest of Heber, near the Mogollon Rim.
Sites: 21 tent and RV up to 16 feet. No hookups.
Road conditions: Paved, dirt.
Management: Apache-Sitgreaves National Forest, 520-535-4481.
Finding the campground: From Heber, drive 12 miles west on Arizona Highway 260, then turn left on Forest Road 300. Continue 3 miles to the campground.

Description: Located on the historic General Crook Trail not far from the Mogollon Rim, the campground is a good base for exploring the rim country. A network of forest roads provides plenty of riding for mountain bikers. The nearest services are in Heber, and the nearest full services are in Payson.

10 Gentry

Location: About 16 miles southwest of Heber, near the Mogollon Rim.
Sites: 6 tent and RV up to 16 feet. No hookups.
Road conditions: Paved, dirt.

Cool streams splash down the canyons below the Mogollon Rim.

Management: Apache-Sitgreaves National Forest, 520-535-4481.
Finding the campground: From Heber, drive 12 miles west on Arizona Highway 260, then turn left on Forest Road 300. Continue 4 miles to the campground.

Description: This small campground is about a mile down the road from Black Canyon Rim Campground. The nearest services are in Heber, and the nearest full services are in Payson.

11 Fool Hollow Lake Recreation Area

Location: About 2 miles west of Show Low, on Fool Hollow Lake.
Sites: 125 tent and RV. 72 electric, 52 full hookups.
Road conditions: Paved.
Management: Fool Hollow Lake Recreation Area, 520-537-3680.
Finding the campground: From Show Low, drive about 2 miles west on Arizona Highway 260, then turn right.

Description: This large recreation complex in the pines and junipers on the shore of Fool Hollow Lake features a visitor center and hiking trails. The campground has showers and partial hookups. The lake is popular with anglers and boaters. Full services are available in Show Low.

12 Show Low Lake County Park

Location: About 5 miles south of Show Low, on Show Low Lake.
Sites: 75 tent and RV. No hookups.
Road conditions: Paved.
Management: Show Low Lake County Park, 520-537-4126.
Finding the campground: From Show Low, drive about 4 miles southeast on Arizona Highway 260, then turn left onto Show Low Lake Road. Continue less than 1 mile to the campground.

Description: Located right in the middle of the Pinetop-Lakeside community, this campground could hardly be more convenient. Fishing and boating are both available on the lake. Full services are available in Show Low and Pinetop-Lakeside.

13 Lakeside

Location: In Pinetop-Lakeside.
Sites: 83 tent and RV up to 32 feet. No hookups.
Road conditions: Paved.
Management: Apache-Sitgreaves National Forest, 520-368-5111.
Finding the campground: The campground is located on Arizona Highway 260 about 9 miles south of Show Low, in the middle of Pinetop-Lakeside.

Description: The campground is in the midst of the busy summer resort area of Pinetop-Lakeside, which stretches for miles along the highway. Full services are available in Pinetop-Lakeside.

14 Scott Reservoir

Location: In Pinetop-Lakeside, on Scott Reservoir.
Sites: 10 tent.
Road conditions: All-weather dirt.
Management: Apache-Sitgreaves National Forest, 520-368-5111.
Finding the campground: From Pinetop-Lakeside, drive about 2 miles east on Forest Road 45 to the campground.

Description: This small campground is on the west shore of Scott Reservoir on the north side of Pinetop-Lakeside. Full services are available in Pinetop-Lakeside.

15 Los Burros

Location: 25 miles east of Show Low, on the Mogollon Plateau.
Sites: 10 tent and RV up to 22 feet. No hookups.
Road conditions: Paved, dirt.
Management: Apache-Sitgreaves National Forest, 520-368-5111.
Finding the campground: From Show Low, drive 18 miles east on Arizona Highway 260 to McNary, then turn left on Forest Road 224. Go 7 miles to the campground.
Description: This small, remote campground is a good base for exploring the eastern Mogollon Rim country. Mountain bikers can check out the many forest roads. The nearest full services are in Pinetop-Lakeside.

ALPINE

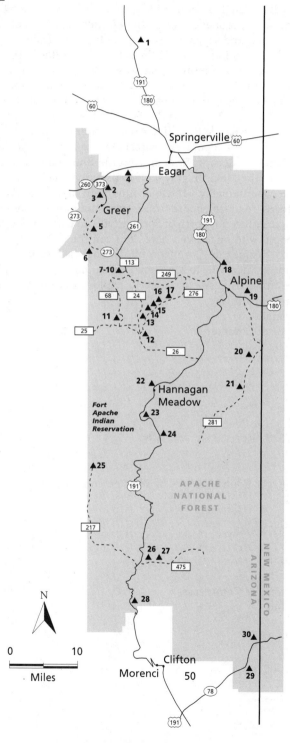

The highest of the High Country stretches across the White Mountains, from the town of Springerville to the hamlet of Alpine near the New Mexico border, and south along the famous Coronado Trail to the old mining towns of Clifton and Morenci. The fir, spruce, and aspen–forested mountains are drained by the headwaters of several rivers, including the Little Colorado, the Black, the White, the Blue, and the San Francisco. These rivers and smaller streams provide some of the state's best stream fishing. And of course there are many mountain lakes, large and small, for boaters and anglers. Wilderness enthusiasts have much to choose from, including the Mount Baldy, Bear Wallow, and Escudilla Wildernesses, and the vast Blue Range Primitive Area. Escudilla Mountain was one of the favorite places of Aldo Leopold, the Forest Service ranger who did much to establish the National Wilderness System. And the Blue Range is the site of an experiment to restore the Mexican gray wolf to its native habitat. If you want to explore the White Mountains by vehicle or mountain bike, you have an extensive network of forest roads to choose from—some maintained, some primitive.

Visit Casa Malpais Museum north of Springerville to learn about the mysterious Mogollon people who once lived here. You can trace the route of Spanish explorer Francisco Vasquez de Coronado by driving the Coronado Trail, U.S. Highway 191, from Springerville to Morenci. During the mid-16th century, Coronado led an expedition from Mexico City to explore the northern reaches of what was then New Spain.

For more information:
Alpine Chamber of Commerce
P.O. Box 410
Alpine, AZ 85920
520-339-4330

Town of Clifton
P.O. Box 1415
Clifton, AZ 85533
520-865-4146

Springerville–Eagar Round Valley Chamber of Commerce
418 E. Main St.
P.O. Box 31
Springerville, AZ 85938
520-333-2123
Fax: 520-333-5690

St. Johns Chamber of Commerce
180 W. Cleveland
P.O. Box 178
St. Johns, AZ 85936
520-337-2000
Fax: 520-337-2000

ALPINE

	Elevation	Season	RV/Trailer	Sites	Drinking Water	Fishing	RV dump	Hiking trails	Boating	Boat launch	Handicap access	Fee ($)	Stay limit (days)
1 Lyman Lake State Park	6,000	All year	•	68	•	•	•	•	•	•		•	14
2 Benney Creek	8,300	May-Oct	•	30	•	•						•	14
3 Rolfe C. Hoyer	8,300	May-Oct	•	100	•	•	•	•			•	•	14
4 South Fork	7,600	May-Nov	•	8		•							14
5 Winn	9,300	May-Oct	•	63	•							•	14
6 Gabaldon	9,400	May-Sep		5				•					14
7 Brook Char	9,100	May-Sep		14	•	•	•		•			•	14
8 Cutthroat	9,100	May-Sep		18	•	•						•	14
9 Grayling	9,200	May-Sep	•	23	•	•						•	14
10 Rainbow	9,200	May-Sep.	•	156	•	•	•	•	•	•		•	14
11 West Fork	7,740	May-Oct		60	•	•							14
12 Buffalo Crossing	7,600	May-Oct	•	20	•	•							14
13 Horse Spring	8,000	May-Oct	•	33	•	•					•	•	14
14 Raccoon	7,600	May-Oct	•	10	•	•							14
15 Deer Creek	7,645	May-Oct	•	6	•	•							14
16 Aspen	7,780	May-Oct		6	•	•							14
17 Diamond Rock	7,900	May-Oct	•	12	•	•							14
18 Alpine Divide	8,500	May-Oct	•	12	•						•	•	14
19 Luna Lake	8,000	May-Sep	•	50	•	•			•	•		•	14
20 Upper Blue	6,200	All year	•	3	•								14
21 Blue Crossing	6,200	All year	•	4		•		•					14
22 Hannagan	9,100	May-Oct	•	8	•			•					14
23 KP Cienega	9,000	May-Sep	•	5	•			•					14
24 Strayhorse	8,200	Apr-Nov	•	7	•			•					14
25 Honeymoon	5,600	Apr-Dec	•	4		•					•		14
26 Upper Juan Miller	6,100	All year	•	4									14
27 Lower Juan Miller	6,000	All year	•	4									14
28 Granville	6,600	Apr-Nov	•	11	•								14
29 Black Jack	6,300	All year	•	10									14
30 Coal Creek	5,900	All year	•	5									14

1 Lyman Lake State Park

Location: About 14 miles north of Springerville, on Lyman Lake.
Sites: 68 tent and RV. 25 water and electric hookups.
Road conditions: Paved.
Management: Lyman Lake State Park, 520-337-4441.

Mount Baldy, Arizona's second highest mountain, looms above the apline valleys at its foot.

Finding the campground: From Springerville, go 13 miles north on U.S. Highway 180/191, then turn right and continue 1 mile to the park.

Description: Lyman Lake is a reservoir on the Little Colorado River in the high desert grasslands of eastern Arizona. It is popular with anglers and boaters. Partial hookups are available, as are showers. There is a group camping area. Due to the elevation, temperatures are tolerable in summer, though summer weekends are busy. Winter is cold and windy; the best seasons are spring and fall. The nearest services are in St. Johns and in Springerville.

2 Benney Creek

Location: About 15 miles southwest of Springerville, in the White Mountains.
Sites: 30 tent and RV up to 24 feet. No hookups.
Road conditions: Paved.
Management: Apache-Sitgreaves National Forest, 520-333-4372.
Finding the campground: From Springerville, drive 12 miles west on Arizona Highway 260, then turn left on AZ 373. Continue 2.5 miles to the campground on the left.

Description: This medium-sized campground in the alpine forest near Greer is popular with anglers, who fish nearby Greer Lakes. Limited supplies are available in Greer; the nearest full services are in Eagar and Springerville.

3 Rolfe C. Hoyer

Location: 15 miles southwest of Springerville, in the White Mountains.
Sites: 100 tent and RV up to 45 feet. No hookups.
Road conditions: Paved.
Management: Apache-Sitgreaves National Forest, 520-333-4372.
Finding the campground: From Springerville, drive 12 miles west on Arizona Highway 260, then turn left on AZ 373. Continue 3 miles to the campground on the right.

Description: This is the main campground at Greer Lakes. Limited supplies are available in Greer; the nearest full services are in Eagar and Springerville.

4 South Fork

Location: About 10 miles southwest of Springerville, in the White Mountains.
Sites: 8 tent and RV up to 32 feet. No hookups.
Road conditions: Paved, dirt.
Management: Apache-Sitgreaves National Forest, 520-333-4372.
Finding the campground: From Springerville, drive 7 miles west on Arizona Highway 260, then turn left on Forest Road 560. Continue 2.5 miles to the campground.

Description: This small campground is located on the South Fork Little Colorado River just inside the forest boundary. Trout fishing is popular on the river. The nearest services are in Eagar and Springerville.

5 Winn

Location: About 30 miles southwest of Springerville, in the White Mountains.
Sites: 63 tent and RV up to 40 feet. No hookups.
Road conditions: Paved, all-weather dirt.
Management: Apache-Sitgreaves National Forest, 520-333-4372.
Finding the campground: From Springerville, drive 5 miles west on Arizona Highway 260, then turn left on AZ 261. Continue 18 miles, then turn right onto AZ 273. Go 6 miles, then turn right on Forest Road 554 and continue 1 mile to the campground.

Description: This large campground makes a good base to explore the nearby Mount Baldy country of the White Mountains. It's also popular with anglers who fish for trout in the mountain streams and lakes. A group campground is available. The nearest services are in Eagar and Springerville.

6 Gabaldon

Location: About 27 miles southwest of Springerville, in the White Mountains.
Sites: 5 tent.

Road conditions: Paved, all-weather dirt.
Management: Apache-Sitgreaves National Forest, 520-333-4372.
Finding the campground: From Springerville, drive 5 miles west on Arizona Highway 260, then turn left on Arizona Highway 261. Continue 18 miles, then turn right onto Arizona Highway 273. Go 4 miles to the campground, which is on the left.

Description: This small campground is close to several trailheads at the edge of the Mount Baldy Wilderness, so it is popular with hikers and equestrians. The nearest services are in Eagar and Springerville.

7 Brook Char

Location: 26 miles southwest of Springerville, in the White Mountains at Big Lake.
Sites: 14 tent.
Road conditions: Paved.
Management: Apache-Sitgreaves National Forest, 520-333-4372.
Finding the campground: From Springerville, drive 5 miles west on Arizona Highway 260, then turn left on AZ 261. Continue 18 miles, then turn left on Forest Road 113. Go 2 miles, then turn right on FR 115 and continue 1 mile to the campground.

Description: This is one of several campgrounds on the shore of Big Lake. As the name implies, Big Lake is the largest in the White Mountains. This beautiful alpine lake, set in rolling meadows scattered with patches of fir and spruce forests, is understandably popular with boaters and anglers. These campgrounds are best avoided on summer weekends. Fall can be perfect, as the mountainsides become slashed with golden aspens. The area is closed by large amounts of snow during winter and spring. Limited supplies are available at the lake. The nearest services are in Eagar and Springerville.

8 Cutthroat

Location: 26 miles southwest of Springerville, in the White Mountains at Big Lake.
Sites: 18 tent.
Road conditions: Paved.
Management: Apache-Sitgreaves National Forest, 520-333-4372.
Finding the campground: From Springerville, drive 5 miles west on Arizona Highway 260, then turn left on AZ 261. Continue 18 miles, then turn left on Forest Road 113. Go 2 miles, then turn right on FR 115 and continue 1 mile to the campground.

Description: This is another campground on the shore of Big Lake. Limited supplies are available at the lake. The nearest services are in Eagar and Springerville.

9 Grayling

Location: 26 miles southwest of Springerville, in the White Mountains at Big Lake.
Sites: 23 tent and RV up to 40 feet. No hookups.
Road conditions: Paved.
Management: Apache-Sitgreaves National Forest, 520-333-4372.
Finding the campground: From Springerville, drive 5 miles west on Arizona Highway 260, then turn left on AZ 261. Continue 18 miles, then turn left on Forest Road 113. Go 2 miles, then turn right on Forest Road 115 and continue 1 mile to the campground.

Description: This is another campground on the shore of Big Lake. Limited supplies are available at the lake. The nearest services are in Eagar and Springerville.

10 Rainbow

Location: 26 miles southwest of Springerville, in the White Mountains at Big Lake.
Sites: 156 tent and RV up to 32 feet. No hookups.
Road conditions: Paved.
Management: Apache-Sitgreaves National Forest, 520-333-4372.
Finding the campground: From Springerville, drive 5 miles west on Arizona Highway 260, then turn left on Arizona Highway 261. Continue 18 miles, then turn left on Forest Road 113. Go 2 miles, then turn right on Forest Road 115 and continue 1 mile to the campground.

Description: This is the largest of the campgrounds on the shore of Big Lake. This campground features a nature trail and a visitor center. Limited supplies are available at the lake. The nearest services are in Eagar and Springerville.

11 West Fork

Location: About 31 miles southwest of Alpine, in the White Mountains.
Sites: 60 tent.
Road conditions: Paved, dirt.
Management: Apache-Sitgreaves National Forest, 520-339-4384.
Finding the campground: From Alpine, drive 14 miles south on U.S. Highway 191, then turn right on Forest Road 26. Continue 9 miles, then turn right on FR 24. Go 3 miles, then turn left onto FR 25. Go 3.5 miles, then turn right on FR 68. Continue 2 miles to the campground.

Description: Located on the West Fork Black River, this is another campground popular with anglers. Campsites are undeveloped. Limited services are available in Alpine; full services are available in Eagar and Springerville.

12 Buffalo Crossing

Location: 26 miles southwest of Alpine, in the White Mountains.
Sites: 20 tent and RV up to 20 feet. No hookups.
Road conditions: Paved, all-weather dirt.
Management: Apache-Sitgreaves National Forest, 520-339-4384.
Finding the campground: From Alpine, drive 14 miles south on U.S. Highway 191, then turn right on Forest Road 26. Continue 9 miles, then turn right on FR 24. Go 3 miles to the campground.

Description: This small campground is very popular with anglers because of its location on the East Fork Black River, a trout stream. It is also a good base for exploring the southern part of the White Mountains. Limited services are available in Alpine; full services are available in Eagar and Springerville.

13 Horse Spring

Location: About 28 miles southwest of Alpine, in the White Mountains.
Sites: 33 tent and RV up to 32 feet. No hookups.
Road conditions: Paved, all-weather dirt.
Management: Apache-Sitgreaves National Forest, 520-339-4384.
Finding the campground: From Alpine, drive 14 miles south on U.S. Highway 191, then turn right on Forest Road 26. Continue 9 miles, then turn right on FR 24. Go 3 miles, then turn right on FR 276 and continue 2 miles to the campground.

Description: This is a medium-sized campground near the East Fork Black River. It is a good base for exploring the southern part of the White Mountains. Limited services are available in Alpine; full services are available in Eagar and Springerville.

14 Raccoon

Location: About 11 miles southwest of Alpine, in the White Mountains.
Sites: 10 tent and RV. No hookups.
Road conditions: Paved, all-weather dirt.
Management: Apache-Sitgreaves National Forest, 520-339-4384.
Finding the campground: From Alpine, drive 14 miles south on U.S. Highway 191, then turn right on Forest Road 26. Continue 9 miles, then turn right on FR 24. Go 3 miles, then turn right on FR 276 and continue about 4 miles to the campground.

Description: This is a small campground on the East Fork Black River. It is also a good base for exploring the southern part of the White Mountains. Limited services are available in Alpine; full services are available in Eagar and Springerville.

15 Deer Creek

Location: About 11 miles southwest of Alpine, in the White Mountains.
Sites: 6 tent and RV. No hookups.
Road conditions: Paved, all-weather dirt.
Management: Apache-Sitgreaves National Forest, 520-339-4384.
Finding the campground: From Alpine, drive 14 miles south on U.S. Highway 191, then turn right on Forest Road 26. Continue 9 miles, then turn right on FR 24. Go 3 miles, then turn right on FR 276 and continue about 4 miles to the campground.

Description: This is another small campground on the East Fork Black River. It is also a good base for exploring the southern part of the White Mountains. Limited services are available in Alpine; full services are available in Eagar and Springerville.

16 Aspen

Location: About 11 miles southwest of Alpine, in the White Mountains.
Sites: 6 tent.
Road conditions: Paved, all-weather dirt.
Management: Apache-Sitgreaves National Forest, 520-339-4384.
Finding the campground: From Alpine, drive 14 miles south on U.S. Highway 191, then turn right on Forest Road 26. Continue 9 miles, then turn right on FR 24. Go 3 miles, then turn right on FR 276 and continue about 5 miles to the campground.

Description: This is yet another small campground on the East Fork Black River. It is also a good base for exploring the southern part of the White Mountains. Limited services are available in Alpine; full services are available in Eagar and Springerville.

17 Diamond Rock

Location: About 13 miles southwest of Alpine, in the White Mountains.
Sites: 12 tent and RV up to 10 feet. No hookups.
Road conditions: Paved, all-weather dirt.
Management: Apache-Sitgreaves National Forest, 520-339-4384.
Finding the campground: From Alpine, drive 14 miles south on U.S. Highway 191, then turn right on Forest Road 26. Continue 9 miles, then turn right on FR 24. Go 3 miles, then turn right on FR 276 and continue about 7 miles to the campground.

Description: This is another small campground on the East Fork Black River. It is also a good base for exploring the southern part of the White Mountains. Limited services are available in Alpine; full services are available in Eagar and Springerville.

18 Alpine Divide

Location: About 4 miles north of Alpine, in the White Mountains.
Sites: 12 tent and RV up to 16 feet. No hookups.
Road conditions: Paved.
Management: Apache-Sitgreaves National Forest, 520-339-4384.
Finding the campground: From Alpine, drive 4 miles north on U.S. Highway 180/191. The campground is on the right.

Description: This small campground is set in the alpine forest right next to the highway, so it is not only in a beautiful setting, it is convenient as well. But do not expect to find space on a summer weekend. It is a good base for exploring nearby Escudilla Mountain, the second highest in the White Mountains. Limited services are available in Alpine; full services are available in Eagar and Springerville.

19 Luna Lake

Location: About 6 miles east of Alpine, in the White Mountains.
Sites: 50 tent and RV up to 32 feet. No hookups.
Road conditions: Paved, all-weather dirt.
Management: Apache-Sitgreaves National Forest, 520-339-4384.
Finding the campground: From Alpine, drive 4 miles east on U.S. Highway 180, then turn left on Forest Road 570. Continue 2 miles to the campground.

Description: Luna Lake is a reservoir on the San Francisco River, and the campground is pleasantly located on its northeast shore. A group campground is available by reservation. A handicap-accessible fishing dock, picnic area, and restroom are located adjacent to the public boat launch ramp on the south shore of the lake. Limited services are available in Alpine; full services are available in Eagar and Springerville.

20 Upper Blue

Location: About 15 miles south of Alpine, on the Blue River.
Sites: 3 tent and RV up to 16 feet. No hookups.
Road conditions: Paved, all-weather dirt.
Management: Apache-Sitgreaves National Forest, 520-339-4384.
Finding the campground: From Alpine, drive 3 miles east on U.S. Highway 180, then turn right on Forest Road 281. Continue 14 miles to the campground, which is on the right.

Description: This tiny campground will mainly be of interest to hikers headed into the nearby Blue Range Primitive Area. Limited services are available in Alpine; full services are available in Eagar and Springerville.

Alpine meadows and quaking aspen grace the high country on Escudilla Mountain.

21 Blue Crossing

Location: About 21 miles south of Alpine, on the Blue River.
Sites: 4 tent and RV up to 16 feet. No hookups.
Road conditions: Paved, dirt.
Management: Apache-Sitgreaves National Forest, 520-339-4384.
Finding the campground: From Alpine, drive 3 miles east on U.S. Highway 180, then turn right on Forest Road 281. Continue 20 miles, then turn right on Forest Road 567, and go 0.1 mile to the campground. During high-water events, common in spring, the campground may not be accessible.

Description: This small campground is mainly of interest to those who wish to fish the Blue River, and to hikers headed into the nearby Blue Range Primitive Area. Limited services are available in Alpine; full services are available in Eagar and Springerville.

22 Hannagan

Location: About 22 miles south of Alpine, in the White Mountains.
Sites: 8 tent and RV up to 16 feet. No hookups.
Road conditions: Paved.
Management: Apache-Sitgreaves National Forest, 520-339-4384.
Finding the campground: From Alpine, drive 23 miles south on U.S. Highway 191. The campground is on the right.

KP Cienega Campground, near Hannagan Meadow in the White Mountains.

Description: This small campground will mainly appeal to those headed into the backcountry—either the Bear Wallow Wilderness or the Blue Range Primitive Area. A livestock corral is available at Hannagan Trailhead, 0.5 mile east of the campground. Limited services are available in Hannagan Meadow and in Alpine; full services are available in Eagar and Springerville.

23 KP Cienega

Location: About 26 miles south of Alpine, in the White Mountains.
Sites: 5 tent and RV up to 16 feet. No hookups.
Road conditions: Paved.
Management: Apache-Sitgreaves National Forest, 520-339-4384.
Finding the campground: From Alpine, drive 28 miles south on U.S. Highway 191, then turn left on Forest Road 155. Continue about 2 miles to the campground.

Description: This small campground is handy for those headed into the backcountry—either the Bear Wallow Wilderness or the Blue Range Primitive Area. Limited services are available in Hannagan Meadow and in Alpine; full services are available in Eagar and Springerville.

24 Strayhorse

Location: About 31 miles south of Alpine.
Sites: 7 tent and RV up to 16 feet. No hookups.
Road conditions: Paved.
Management: Apache-Sitgreaves National Forest, 520-687-1301.
Finding the campground: From Alpine, drive 31 miles south on U.S. Highway 191.

Description: This small campground mainly appeals to those who wish to explore the many hiking trails in the area, including routes into the Blue Range Primitive Area and Bear Wallow Wilderness. It is also a convenient stop for those who drive the historic Coronado Trail. Limited services are available in Hannagan Meadow and Alpine; full services are available in Eagar and Springerville.

25 Honeymoon

Location: About 45 miles north of Clifton, along Eagle Creek.
Sites: 4 tent and RV up to 16 feet. No hookups.
Road conditions: Paved, dirt.
Management: Apache-Sitgreaves National Forest, 520-687-1301.
Finding the campground: From Clifton, drive 25 miles north on U.S. Highway 191, then turn left on Forest Road 217. Continue 20 miles to the campground.

Description: This tiny and remote campground is convenient for those who wish to fish Eagle Creek, and to explore the area. Limited services are available in Clifton; full services are available in Safford.

26 Upper Juan Miller

Location: About 27 miles north of Clifton, near the Coronado Trail.
Sites: 4 tent.
Road conditions: Paved, dirt.
Management: Apache-Sitgreaves National Forest, 520-687-1301.
Finding the campground: From Clifton, drive 26 miles north on U.S. Highway 191, then turn right on Forest Road 475. Continue less than a mile to the campground.

Description: This is one of two small campgrounds located together near the Coronado Trail, U.S. Highway 191. It is a convenient stop for those who drive the historic route, and also a good base for those exploring the backcountry. Limited services are available in Clifton, and full services are available in Safford.

27 Lower Juan Miller

Location: About 28 miles north of Clifton, near the Coronado Trail.
Sites: 4 tent and RV up to 16 feet. No hookups.
Road conditions: Paved, dirt.
Management: Apache-Sitgreaves National Forest, 520-687-1301.
Finding the campground: From Clifton, drive 26 miles north on U.S. Highway 191, then turn right on Forest Road 475. Continue about 1.5 miles to the campground.

Description: This is one of two small campgrounds located together near the Coronado Trail. Limited services are available in Clifton, and full services are available in Safford.

28 Granville

Location: 18 miles north of Clifton, along the Coronado Trail.
Sites: 11 tent and RV up to 16 feet. No hookups.
Road conditions: Paved.
Management: Apache-Sitgreaves National Forest, 520-687-1301.
Finding the campground: From Clifton, drive 18 miles north on U.S. Highway 191.

Description: This is another convenient stop for those exploring the historic Coronado Trail, and also a good base for those exploring the backcountry. Limited services are available in Clifton; full services are available in Safford.

29 Black Jack

Location: About 23 miles southeast of Clifton, in the Big Lue Mountains.
Sites: 10 tent and RV up to 16 feet. No hookups.
Road conditions: Paved.

Management: Apache-Sitgreaves National Forest, 520-687-1301.
Finding the campground: From Clifton, drive 9 miles south on U.S. Highway 191, then turn left on Arizona Highway 78. Continue about 14 miles to the campground.

Description: This small campground mainly appeals to those campers passing through on the highway. It can also serve as a base for exploring the Big Lue Mountains. Limited services are available in Clifton, and full services are available in Safford.

30 Coal Creek

Location: About 27 miles southeast of Clifton, in the Big Lue Mountains.
Sites: 5 tent and RV up to 16 feet. No hookups.
Road conditions: Paved.
Management: Apache-Sitgreaves National Forest, 520-687-1301.
Finding the campground: From Clifton, drive 9 miles south on U.S. Highway 191, then turn left on Arizona Highway 78. Continue about 18 miles to the campground.

Description: This small campground is also handy for those campers passing through on the highway. It can also serve as a base for exploring the Big Lue Mountains. There are limited services in Clifton, and full services in Safford.

Old West Country

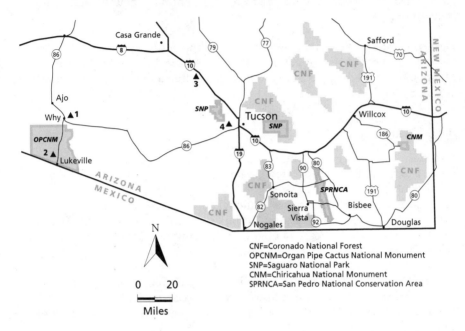

CNF=Coronado National Forest
OPCNM=Organ Pipe Cactus National Monument
SNP=Saguaro National Park
CNM=Chiricahua National Monument
SPRNCA=San Pedro National Conservation Area

Old West Country comprises the grassy valleys and high mountains of southeast Arizona. The forested sky islands of the Coronado National Forest are home to a diverse and unique mix of plant and animal species from the Rocky Mountains to the north, and the Sierra Madre to the south, in Mexico. Campgrounds abound in the mountains and in the deserts, and there is a wide range of outdoor activities to tempt you, including rock climbing, hiking, fishing, mountain biking, and exploring back roads.

Known as Old West Country because of its rich western heritage, the region's cultural history started with the Native Americans who made this beautiful area their home. When Europeans entered the area, they soon encountered fierce resistance from the Apache, who hid in the rugged mountains and carried out daring raids on the invaders. Starting in the mid-16th century, Spanish explorers roamed the area and soon made it part of the Spanish Empire in the New World, with Tucson as the capital. The Spanish legacy remains in the form of missions and its deep influence on the culture of the area. When southern Arizona became part of the United States 150 years ago, American cowboys and ranchers began to move into the area, attracted by the rich grasslands. Led by famous chiefs such as Cochise and Geronimo, the Chiricahua Apache continued to resist until Geronimo's surrender in 1886.

TUCSON

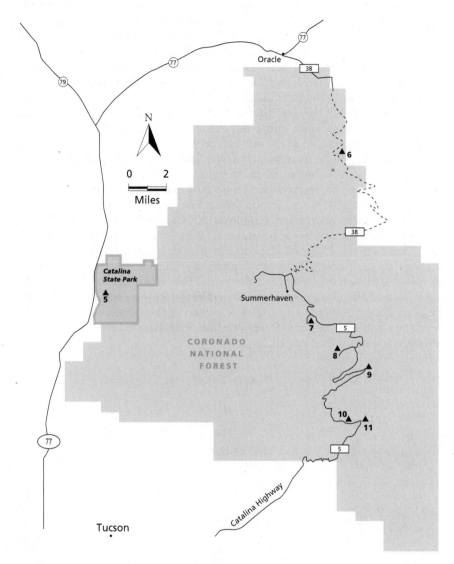

Still known as the Old Pueblo, the city of Tucson is the cultural center of south-eastern Arizona. This desert city is surrounded by bold mountains that rise dra-matically from the beautiful Sonoran desert foothills to the craggy, forested summits. Organ Pipe Cactus National Monument, to the southwest, preserves a unique sample of the Sonoran desert containing the rare Organ Pipe cactus and many other unique plants and animals. Closer to the city, the Tucson Mountains contain Saguaro National Park West, which protects one of the largest stands of giant cactus in the world. Visit the nearby Arizona-Sonora Desert Museum, which has a large and diverse collection of desert plants and animals, many in natural settings. Saguaro National Park East is set in the Rincon Mountains, a chunk of wilderness backcountry that varies from saguaro cactus forest to pine and fir-covered mountain peaks. North of Tucson, the Santa Catalina Mountains also range from desert to forest, and you can drive from one to the other in a short time on the Catalina Highway. The road ends near the 9,157-foot summit of Mount Lemmon, site of a summer home community and the southernmost alpine ski area in the United States Campgrounds are scattered along the Catalina Highway, as well as in the foothills. Backcountry hikers can spend days exploring the rugged Pusch Ridge and Rincon Wildernesses. The Catalinas are famous among rock climbers for the varied and challenging routes found here.

Tucson has a reputation as the cultural center of Arizona, and you won't be disappointed. You might want to start with the Arizona Historical Society Tucson Museum. Aviation buffs will be in paradise at the Pima Air Museum. If you're a fan of fine photography, don't miss the Center for Creative Photography on the University of Arizona campus, which houses work by famous photographers such as Ansel Adams and Eugene Smith. Children will enjoy the Tucson Children's Museum, which has hands-on exhibits. Want to learn more about the stars? Check out the Flandrau Planetarium, also on campus. It features regular programs on the heavens. You can explore the Spanish history of the area at several sites, including Mission San Xavier del Bac, which has been dubbed the White Dove of the Desert for its classic, white stucco–covered adobe architecture. Tumacacori National Historic Park preserves the remains of another important Spanish mission, and Tubac Presidio State Historic Park preserves an important Spanish military post.

For more information:

Ajo Chamber of Commerce
321 Taladro
Ajo, AZ 85321
520-387-7742

Metro Tucson Convention & Visitors Bureau
130 S. Scott Ave.
Tucson, AZ 85701
520-624-1817
800-638-8350
Fax: 520-884-7804

TUCSON

		Elevation	Season	RV/Trailer	Sites	Drinking Water	Fishing	RV dump	Hiking trails	Boating	Boat launch	Handicap access	Fee ($)	Stay limit (days)
1	Coyote Howls Park	1,783	All year	•	550	•		•	•				•	
2	Organ Pipe Cactus National Monument	1,800	All year	•	208	•		•	•			•	•	14
3	Picacho Peak State Park	2,000	All year	•	95	•			•			•	•	14
4	Gilbert Ray	3,100	All year	•	149	•		•					•	7
5	Catalina State Park	2,650	All year	•	50	•		•	•			•	•	14
6	Peppersauce	4,700	All year	•	17	•							•	14
7	Spencer Canyon	7,600	Apr-Oct	•	62	•						•	•	14
8	Rose Canyon	7,200	Apr-Oct	•	74	•	•		•			•	•	14
9	General Hitchcock	6,000	Apr-Oct		12							•	•	11
10	Prison Camp	4,800	All year	•	8							•	•	14
11	Molino	4,500	Oct-Apr	•	34							•	•	14

1 Coyote Howls Park

Location: About 111 miles west of Tucson, at the town of Why. (This campground is shown on the "Old West Country" map.)
Sites: 550 tent and RV.
Road conditions: Paved.
Management: Town of Why, 520-387-5209.
Finding the campground: From Tucson, drive 111 miles west on Arizona Highway 86 to the town of Why at the junction with AZ 85.

Description: This is a good alternate to the campground at Organ Pipe Cactus National Monument. Popular with winter visitors, this campground is a good starting point for exploring the national monument and the surrounding Sonoran desert. Limited services are available in Lukeville, Why, and Ajo; the nearest full services are in Tucson and Phoenix.

2 Organ Pipe Cactus National Monument

Location: About 130 miles west of Tucson, in Organ Pipe Cactus National Monument. (This campground is shown on the "Old West Country" map.)
Sites: 208 tent and RV up to 35 feet. No hookups.
Road conditions: Paved.
Management: Organ Pipe Cactus National Monument, 520-387-6849.
Finding the campground: From Tucson, drive 111 miles west on Arizona Highway 86, then turn left and go about 20 miles south on Arizona Highway 85. Turn right into the visitor center, and follow the signs to the campground.

Description: Popular with winter visitors and travelers, the monument campground is located in a unique area of the Sonoran desert. Nearby activities include scenic drives and hiking trails. The visitor center is a good place to begin exploring the monument. Limited services are available in Lukeville, Why, and Ajo; the nearest full services are in Tucson and Phoenix.

3 Picacho Peak State Park

Location: About 40 miles northwest of Tucson, along Interstate 10. (This campground is shown on the "Old West Country" map.)
Sites: 95 tent and RV. 10 water and electric hookups.
Road conditions: Paved.
Management: Picacho Peak State Park, 520-466-3183.
Finding the campground: From Tucson, go 40 miles west on Interstate 10, and exit at Picacho Peak.

Description: This desert campground at the base of spectacular Picacho Peak features nature trails and hiking trails. Some partial hookups are provided. Group camping is available by reservation. Showers are available. Limited services are available nearby; the nearest full services are in Casa Grande and Tucson.

Pima Canyon tumbles from the forested heights of the Santa Catalina Mountains.

4 Gilbert Ray

Location: About 10 miles west of Tucson, in the Tucson Mountains. (This campground is shown on the "Old West Country" map.)
Sites: 149 tent and RV up to 30 feet. Electric hookups.
Road conditions: Paved.
Management: Tucson Mountain Park, 520-883-4200.
Finding the campground: From Tucson on Interstate 10, exit at Speedway Boulevard Go west; the road becomes Gates Pass Road. After 10 miles, turn left into the campground access road.

Description: This desert campground is an ideal base from which to explore nearby Saguaro National Park, which has no campgrounds. Summers are too hot here, and not all campground facilities are open then, but fall, winter, and spring are delightful. In wet years, the desert becomes a riot of wildflowers in the spring. Full services are available in Tucson.

5 Catalina State Park

Location: About 8 miles north of Tucson, at the foot of the Santa Catalina Mountains.
Sites: 50 tent and RV. No hookups.
Road conditions: Paved.
Management: Catalina State Park, 520-628-5798.
Finding the campground: From Tucson, drive north on Arizona Highway 77. The park is 8 miles north of Ina Road.

Description: This is a desert campground and park adjacent to the Coronado National Forest. Nature, hiking, and equestrian trails are available in the park and in the national forest. Showers and partial hookups are provided. Equestrian and group facilities are also available. Full services are available in Tucson.

6 Peppersauce

Location: About 38 miles northeast of Tucson, on the northeast slopes of the Santa Catalina Mountains.
Sites: 17 tent and RV up to 22 feet. No hookups.
Road conditions: Paved, dirt.
Management: Coronado National Forest, 520-749-8700.
Finding the campground: From Tucson, drive about 30 miles north on Arizona Highway 77 to Oracle, then turn right on American Avenue (Forest Road 38). Continue 8 miles to the campground.

Description: This remote campground is located in the northeastern foothills of the Santa Catalina Mountains. Its low elevation keeps the campground open all year. It is a good base for exploring the remote northern sections of the Catalinas. A small group area is available for up to 50 people. The nearest services are in Oracle, and the nearest full services are in Tucson.

7 Spencer Canyon

Location: About 22 miles northeast of Tucson, in the Santa Catalina Mountains.
Sites: 62 tent and RV up to 22 feet. No hookups.
Road conditions: Paved.
Management: Coronado National Forest, 520-749-8700.
Finding the campground: From Tucson, drive northeast on the Catalina Highway, Forest Road 5, to Milepost 21.6, and turn left onto the campground access road.

Description: Located high in the Santa Catalina Mountains in pine forest, this is one of several mountain campgrounds that provides a cool retreat from the desert below. It is also a good base for exploring the mountains, including the nearby Pusch Ridge Wilderness. Expect the campground to fill rapidly on summer weekends. There are two group areas that accommodate 15 people each. More group camping is available at Showers Point Group Campground, about 2 miles to the south. Limited services are in Summerhaven; the nearest full services are in Tucson.

8 Rose Canyon

Location: About 16 miles northeast of Tucson, in the Santa Catalina Mountains.
Sites: 74 tent and RV up to 22 feet. No hookups.
Road conditions: Paved.
Management: Coronado National Forest, 520-749-8700.
Finding the campground: From Tucson, drive northeast on the Catalina Highway, Forest Road 5, to Milepost 16, and turn left onto FR 9, the campground access road.

Description: This is the largest of several mountain campgrounds that provides a cool retreat from the desert below. Fishing is available in nearby Rose Canyon Lake. Expect the campground to fill rapidly on summer weekends. Limited services are in Summerhaven; the nearest full services are in Tucson.

9 General Hitchcock

Location: About 12 miles northeast of Tucson, in the Santa Catalina Mountains.
Sites: 12 tent.
Road conditions: Paved.
Management: Coronado National Forest, 520-749-8700.
Finding the campground: From Tucson, drive northeast on the Catalina Highway, Forest Road 5, to Milepost 12, and turn right onto FR 605, the campground access road.

Description: This is the smallest of the Santa Catalina campgrounds. It has mostly walk-in tent campsites; trailers and RVs are not allowed. Expect the campground to fill rapidly on summer weekends. Limited services are in Summerhaven; the nearest full services are in Tucson.

10 Prison Camp

Location: About 7 miles northeast of Tucson, in the Santa Catalina Mountains.
Sites: 8 tent and RV up to 22 feet. No hookups.
Road conditions: Paved.
Management: Coronado National Forest, 520-749-8700.
Finding the campground: From Tucson, drive northeast on the Catalina Highway, Forest Road 5, to Milepost 7.

Description: Only slightly higher than Molino Campground, this small site is also hot in summer. It is best enjoyed in fall, winter, and spring. Full services are available in Tucson.

11 Molino

Location: About 6 miles northeast of Tucson, in the Santa Catalina Mountains.
Sites: 34 tent and RV up to 22 feet. No hookups.
Road conditions: Paved.
Management: Coronado National Forest, 520-749-8700.
Finding the campground: From Tucson, drive northeast on the Catalina Highway, Forest Road 5, to Milepost 6, and turn right onto the campground access road.

Description: This is the lowest in elevation of the Santa Catalina campgrounds, and it is best in fall, winter, and spring. Full services are available in Tucson.

SAFFORD

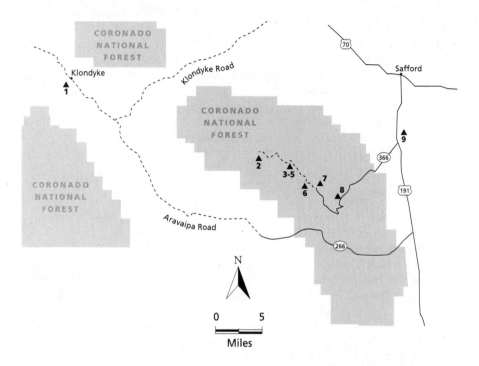

Safford is the center of a thriving ranching community along the Gila River Valley. Towering above the valley, the Pinaleno Mountains and several smaller ranges are the recreational center of the area. Capped by 10,717-foot Mount Graham, the Pinalenos are more than 50 miles long and the summit ridge and north slopes are covered with a dense, cool forest of pine, fir, oak, and aspen. Campgrounds are scattered along the Swift Trail, a road that winds along the high south slopes of the range. There are miles of hiking trails, including the rugged Round the Mountain Trail, and several fishing streams. Other backcountry areas to explore include the wild Santa Teresa and Galiuro Mountains, both included in wilderness areas. In the foothills of the Galiuro, beautiful Aravaipa Canyon winds through green streamside trees. Although outdoor recreation is the main activity for campers, you might want to check out Discovery Park, Safford's 165-acre science and cultural center.

For more information:
Graham County Chamber of Commerce
1111 Thatcher Blvd.
Safford, AZ 85546
520-428-2511
Fax: 520-428-0744

Town of Thatcher
P.O. Box 670
Thatcher, AZ 85552

SAFFORD

		Elevation	Season	RV/Trailer	Sites	Drinking Water	Fishing	RV dump	Hiking trails	Boating	Boat launch	Handicap access	Fee ($)	Stay limit (days)
1	Fourmile Canyon	3,500	All year	•	10	•							•	14
2	Riggs Flat	8,500	May-Oct	•	26	•	•			•			•	14
3	Columbine Corrals	9,600	May-Oct	•	6	•			•				•	14
4	Cunningham	9,000	May-Oct	•	10				•					14
5	Soldier Creek	9,300	May-Oct	•	12	•			•				•	14
6	Hospital Flat	9,000	May-Oct		10	•			•				•	14
7	Shannon	9,100	May-Oct	•	11	•							•	14
8	Arcadia	6,700	All year	•	19	•							•	14
9	Roper Lake State Park	3,130	All year	•	100	•	•	•	•	•	•	•	•	14

1 Fourmile Canyon

Location: About 48 miles west of Safford, in the foothills of the Galiuro Mountains.
Sites: 10 tent and RV up to 30 feet. No hookups.
Road conditions: Paved, all-weather dirt.
Management: Bureau of Land Management, 520-348-4400.
Finding the campground: From Safford, drive west 13.4 miles on U.S. Highway 70, then turn left on Klondyke Road. Continue 32.4 miles to Klondyke, then turn left on Fourmile Canyon Road. Go 0.5 mile to the campground.

Description: This desert campground is a good retreat during the cooler months of fall, winter, and spring. It's also a good base for exploring the nearby Santa Teresa, Galiuro, and Aravaipa Canyon Wildernesses. The nearest full services are in Safford.

2 Riggs Flat

Location: About 40 miles southwest of Safford, in the Pinaleno Mountains.
Sites: 26 tent and RV up to 22 feet. No hookups.
Road conditions: Paved, dirt.
Management: Coronado National Forest, 520-428-4150.
Finding the campground: From Safford, drive 9 miles south on U.S. Highway 191, then turn right on Swift Trail, Arizona Highway 366. Continue about 32 miles to the campground on the left.

Description: Located in the pine and fir forest at the west end of the Swift Trail, this popular spot is the most distant of the Pinaleno campgrounds. Fishing and limited boating are available on nearby Riggs Lake. This is also a good base for exploring the mountains; there are numerous hiking trails in the area. The nearest full services are in Safford.

The Pinaleno Mountains tower over the Gila River Valley.

3 Columbine Corrals

Location: About 40 miles southwest of Safford, in the Pinaleno Mountains.
Sites: 6 tent and RV up to 16 feet. No hookups.
Road conditions: Paved, dirt.
Management: Coronado National Forest, 520-428-4150.
Finding the campground: From Safford, drive 9 miles south on U.S. Highway 191, then turn right on Swift Trail, Arizona Highway 366. Continue about 30 miles to the campground.

Description: Located in the pine and fir forest near the site of old Columbine, this is an equestrian camp with horse facilities and access to trails. The nearest full services are in Safford.

4 Cunningham

Location: About 40 miles southwest of Safford, in the Pinaleno Mountains.
Sites: 10 tent and RV up to 22 feet. No hookups.
Road conditions: Paved, dirt.
Management: Coronado National Forest, 520-428-4150.
Finding the campground: From Safford, drive 9 miles south on U.S. Highway 191, then turn right on Swift Trail, Arizona Highway 366. Continue about 30 miles to the campground.

Description: This is another equestrian camp with horse facilities and access to trails. The nearest full services are in Safford.

5 Soldier Creek

Location: About 37 miles southwest of Safford, in the Pinaleno Mountains.
Sites: 12 tent and RV up to 22 feet. No hookups.
Road conditions: Paved, dirt.
Management: Coronado National Forest, 520-428-4150.
Finding the campground: From Safford, drive 9 miles south on U.S. Highway 191, then turn right on Swift Trail, Arizona Highway 366. Continue about 28 miles to the campground, which is on the left.

Description: This is another campground along the Swift Trail in the old Columbine area. It is a good base for exploring the mountains; there are numerous hiking trails in the area. The nearest full services are in Safford.

6 Hospital Flat

Location: About 31 miles of Safford, in the Pinaleno Mountains.
Sites: 10 tent.
Road conditions: Paved, dirt.
Management: Coronado National Forest, 520-428-4150.

Finding the campground: From Safford, drive 9 miles south on US Highway 191, then turn right on Swift Trail, Arizona Highway 366. Continue about 22 miles to the campground, which is on the left.

Description: This is another small campground along the Swift Trail. This one allows tents only; it is not suitable for trailers or RV's. The nearest full services are in Safford.

7 Shannon

Location: About 30 miles southwest of Safford, in the Pinaleno Mountains.
Sites: 11 tent and RV up to 16 feet. No hookups.
Road conditions: Paved, dirt.
Management: Coronado National Forest, 520-428-4150.
Finding the campground: From Safford, drive 9 miles south on US Highway 191, then turn right on Swift Trail, Arizona Highway 366. Continue about 21 miles to the campground, which is on the right.

Description: This is yet another small campground along the Swift Trail. The nearest full services are in Safford.

8 Arcadia

Location: About 19 miles southwest of Safford, in the Pinaleno Mountains.
Sites: 19 tent and RV up to 22 feet. No hookups.
Road conditions: Paved.
Management: Coronado National Forest, 520-428-4150.
Finding the campground: From Safford, drive 9 miles south on US Highway 191, then turn right on Swift Trail, Arizona Highway 366. Continue about 10 miles to the campground, which is on the right.

Description: This is the lowest of the campgrounds along the Swift Trail in the Pinaleno Mountains, and the only one open all year. Water is available from May through October. The nearest full services are in Safford.

9 Roper Lake State Park

Location: 4 miles south of Safford, at Roper Lake.
Sites: 100 tent and RV. 30 water and electric hookups.
Road conditions: Paved.
Management: Roper Lake State Park, 520-428-6760.
Finding the campground: From Safford, go about 4 miles south on US Highway 191, then turn left into the park.

Description: Although summers are hot, the park is usually busy on summer weekends. Fishing and boating (electric motors only) are popular on the lake. Partial hookups are available. Showers and a group campsite are available. Full services are available in Safford.

NOGALES

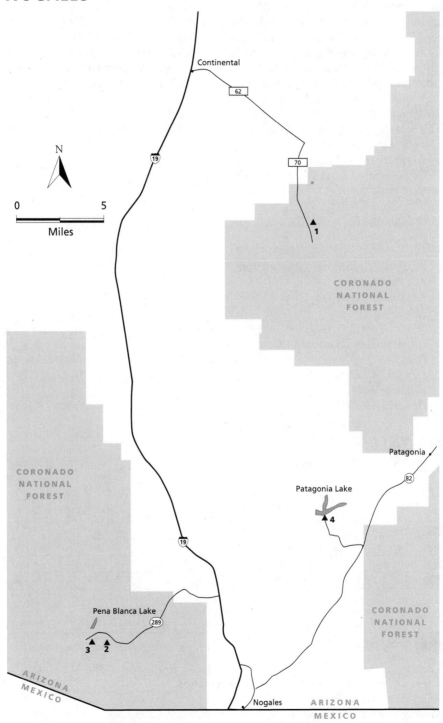

N

0 _____ 5
Miles

Continental

62

19

70

▲ 1

CORONADO
NATIONAL
FOREST

Patagonia

CORONADO
NATIONAL
FOREST

82

Patagonia Lake

▲ 4

19

Pena Blanca Lake

289

CORONADO
NATIONAL
FOREST

▲ ▲
3 2

ARIZONA
MEXICO

Nogales   ARIZONA
MEXICO

Nogales is best known as the entrance to Mexico and the city of Nogales, Sonora. But campers and recreationists have opportunities here, too. The beautiful grass and oak uplands of the Atacosa Mountains offer plenty of opportunities for back road explorations, as well as a lake very popular with anglers. Hikers will want to check out Sycamore Canyon in the Pajarita Wilderness. Classic ranching country surrounds the hamlets of Patagonia and Sonoita. Anglers and boaters have Patagonia Lake, and hikers can spend days in the Mount Wrightson Wilderness high atop the Santa Rita Mountains. If you're a bird watcher, you'll want to visit the Patagonia-Sonoita Creek Preserve, maintained by The Nature Conservancy. This world-famous sanctuary, on a major migration route, hosts over 250 species of birds, including nine varieties of hummingbirds.

For more information:
Nogales/Santa Cruz Chamber of Commerce
Kino Park
Nogales, AZ 85621
520-287-3685
Fax: 520-287-3688

Patagonia Community Association
P.O. Box 241
Patagonia, AZ 85624
520-394-0060

Sonoita/Elgin Chamber of Commerce
Box 264
Sonoita, AZ 85637
520-455-5613
Fax: 520-455-5613

NOGALES

		Elevation	Season	RV/Trailer	Sites	Drinking Water	Fishing	RV dump	Hiking trails	Boating	Boat launch	Handicap access	Fee ($)	Stay limit (days)
1	Bog Springs	5,600	All year	•	13	•							•	14
2	White Rock	4,000	All year	•	15	•							•	14
3	Calebasas	4,000	All year	•	12								•	14
4	Patagonia Lake State Park	4,000	All year	•	82	•	•	•	•	•	•		•	14

1 Bog Springs

Location: About 50 miles northeast of Nogales, in the Santa Rita Mountains.
Sites: 13 tent and RV up to 22 feet. No hookups.
Road conditions: Paved.
Management: Coronado National Forest, 520-281-2296.

Finding the campground: From Nogales, drive 40 miles north on Interstate 19, then exit at Continental. (This exit is 23 miles south of Tucson.) Go 6 miles east on Forest Road 62, then turn right on FR 70, Madera Canyon Road. Continue 4 miles, then turn left on the campground access road.

Description: This small campground is the only one in the Santa Rita Mountains. Because of its low elevation, the campground is open all year. It tends to fill quickly on summer weekends. Madera Canyon is famous among birders for its rare species. The canyon is also popular with hikers who want to climb Mt. Wrightson, or explore the Mt. Wrightson Wilderness. Limited services are available in Continental; the nearest full services are in Tucson.

2 White Rock

Location: About 16 miles northwest of Nogales, in the Atacosa Mountains.
Sites: 15 tent and RV up to 22 feet. No hookups.
Road conditions: Paved.
Management: Coronado National Forest, 520-281-2296.
Finding the campground: From Nogales, drive 7 miles north on Interstate 19, then turn left on Arizona Highway 289. Continue 9 miles west to the campground.

Description: This is one of two small campgrounds near Pena Blanca Lake. The lake is popular with anglers, although the campground could be used as a base to explore the Atacosa Mountains, including the Pajarita Wilderness to the west. The nearest full services are in Nogales.

3 Calebasas

Location: About 16 miles northwest of Nogales, in the Atacosa Mountains.
Sites: 12 tent and RV up to 22 feet. No hookups.
Road conditions: Paved.
Management: Coronado National Forest, 520-281-2296.
Finding the campground: From Nogales, drive 7 miles north on Interstate 19, then turn left on Arizona Highway 289. Continue 9 miles west to the campground.

Description: This is the other small campground near Pena Blanca Lake. The nearest full services are in Nogales.

4 Patagonia Lake State Park

Location: About 16 miles northeast of Nogales, on Patagonia Lake.
Sites: 82 tent and RV up to 35 feet. 10 water and electric hookups.
Road conditions: Paved.
Management: Patagonia Lake State Park, 520-287-6965.
Finding the campground: From Nogales, drive 12 miles north on Arizona High-

An open oak forest in the Atacosa Mountains.

way 82, then turn left on Patagonia Lake Road and continue about 4 miles to the park.

Description: Located in the classic oak and grassland country of south central Arizona, this park is popular year-round. Boating and fishing are very popular on the lake, and weekends are crowded. The park also has hiking trails. On weekdays you can enjoy peaceful sunsets and watch the graceful herons. The campground has showers and a group camping area. Partial hookups are also available. There are 13 boat-only campsites. Limited supplies are available in the park and in Patagonia; the nearest full services are in Nogales.

SIERRA VISTA

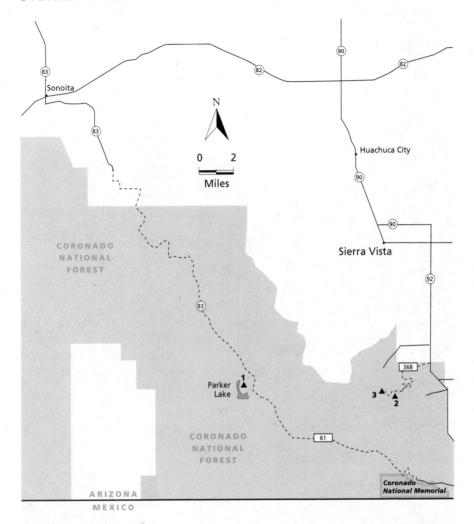

Sierra Vista is a retirement and military community at the base of the Huachuca Mountains. Nearby Fort Huachuca was originally established as an army post during the Apache wars, and now serves as a test site. The fort's museum traces the history of the "Buffalo Soldiers." Parker Canyon Lake, in the Canelo Hills west of the Huachuca Mountains, is popular with boaters and anglers. The Huachucas, in the Coronado National Forest, run northwest to southeast, and culminate in 9,466-foot Miller Peak. The Miller Peak Wilderness is laced with hiking trails, and the Nature Conservancy's Ramsey Canyon Preserve is a legendary site for spotting rare birds. Muleshoe Ranch Preserve, another Nature Conservancy preserve, operated in cooperation with the Bureau of Land Management's San Pedro Riparian National Conservation Area, protects one of the last free-flowing rivers in the state.

Carr Peak in the Huachuca Mountains.

For more information:
Sierra Vista Chamber of Commerce
77 S. Calle Portal #A140
Sierra Vista, AZ 85635
520-458-6940
800-288-3861
Fax: 520-452-0878

SIERRA VISTA

		Elevation	Season	RV/Trailer	Sites	Drinking Water	Fishing	RV dump	Hiking trails	Boating	Boat launch	Handicap access	Fee ($)	Stay limit (days)
1	Lakeview	5,400	All year	•	65	•	•			•			•	14
2	Reef Townsite	7,200	All year	•	14	•							•	14
3	Ramsey Vista	7,200	All year	•	8	•							•	14

1   Lakeview

Location: About 28 miles southeast of Sonoita, at Parker Lake.
Road conditions: Paved, dirt.
Sites: 65 tent and RV up to 32 feet. No hookups.
Management: Coronado National Forest, 520-378-0311.
Finding the campground: From Sonoita, drive 28 miles south and east on Arizona Highway 83 to the campground.

Description: This campground is on the east shore of Parker Lake, a small reservoir. It is popular with boaters and anglers. Though it is open all year, summer weekends tend to be busy. Limited services are available in Sonoita; the nearest full services are in Tucson and Sierra Vista.

2   Reef Townsite

Location: About 14 miles southeast of Sierra Vista, in the Huachuca Mountains.
Sites: 14 tent and RV up to 16 feet. No hookups.
Road conditions: Paved, dirt.
Management: Coronado National Forest, 520-378-0311.
Finding the campground: From Sierra Vista at the junction of Arizona Highways 90 and 92, drive 7 miles south on AZ 92. Turn right on Carr Canyon Road, Forest Road 368, and continue 6.5 miles to the campground.

Description: Located high in the Huachuca Mountains near the old Reef Townsite, this campground is 2,500 feet higher than Sierra Vista and is correspondingly cooler. Though open all year, winter can bring snow and cold temperatures. The view of the surrounding mountains is superb, partially because a series of forest fires have burned many of the large trees in the basin. The campground is a good base for exploring trails into the nearby Miller Peak Wilderness. A group campground is available. The nearest full services are in Sierra Vista.

3 Ramsey Vista

Location: About 14 miles southeast of Sierra Vista, in the Huachuca Mountains.
Sites: 8 tent and RV up to 16 feet. No hookups.
Road conditions: Paved, dirt.
Management: Coronado National Forest, 520-378-0311.
Finding the campground: From Sierra Vista at the junction of Arizona Highways 90 and 92, drive 7 miles south on AZ 92. Turn right on Carr Canyon Road, Forest Road 368, and continue 7 miles to the end of the road.

Description: See Reef Townsite Campground for details on this area. The nearest services are in Sierra Vista.

DOUGLAS

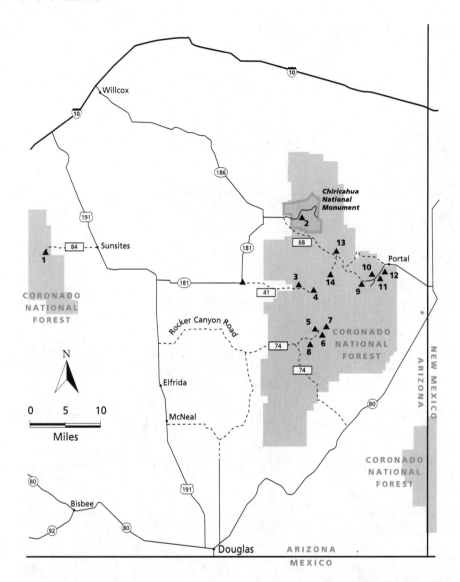

Douglas (in the southeastern corner of the state on the Mexican border) Willcox to the north, and Bisbee to the west frame several sky island mountain ranges with plenty of camping and recreational activities. Cochise Stronghold in the granite-cragged Dragoon Mountains was the last holdout of the famous Chiricahua Apache leader and his band of warriors and their families. The Chiricahua Mountains, a 9,000-foot range crowned with a Rocky Mountain forest of pine and fir, features the Chiricahua Wilderness and many miles of wilderness trails. The north end of the range features stone hoodoos—a wonderland of volcanic rock—protected in Chiricahua National Monument. Nearby Fort Bowie

Easy hiking trails lead through a forest of stone hoodoos in Chiricahua National Monument.

was a post for army soldiers engaged in the desperate fight against the Apache in the last century. Western history fans have to visit Tombstone, the "town too tough to die." One of the rowdiest of western mining towns, it was the scene of the famous "shootout at the OK Corral," where famous and obscure gunslingers faced off, guns blazing. The losers died with their boots on and were buried in nearby Boot Hill.

For more information:

Douglas Chamber of Commerce
1125 Pan American Ave.
Douglas, AZ 85607
520-364-2477
Fax: 520-364-6535

Duncan Visitors Center
P.O. Box 814
123 Railroad Blvd.
Duncan, AZ 85534

Sulphur Springs Valley Chamber of Commerce
P.O. Box 614
Elfrida, AZ 85610

Tombstone Chamber of Commerce & Visitor Center
Box 995
4th & Fremont
Tombstone, AZ 85638
520-457-9317
520-457-3929
Fax: 520-457-3929

Willcox Chamber of Commerce
1500 North Circle I Rd.
Willcox, AZ 85643
520-384-2272
800-200-2272
Fax: 520-384-0293

DOUGLAS

		Elevation	Season	RV/Trailer	Sites	Drinking Water	Fishing	RV dump	Hiking trails	Boating	Boat launch	Handicap access	Fee ($)	Stay limit (days)
1	Cochise Stronghold	5,000	All year	•	18	•			•				•	14
2	Bonita	5,400	All year	•	26	•			•				•	14
3	West Turkey Creek	5,900	All year	•	4				•					14
4	Sycamore	6,200	All year	•	5									14
5	Bathtub	6,400	Mar-Oct		11	•			•				•	14
6	Rucker Forest Camp	6,500	Mar-Oct	•	14	•			•				•	14
7	Rucker Lake	6,300	Mar-Oct	•	8	•			•				•	14
8	Cypress Park	6,000	Mar-Oct		7	•			•				•	14
9	Herb Martyr	5,800	All year		5				•					14
10	Sunny Flat	5,200	All year	•	11	•			•				•	14
11	Stewart	5,100	Mar-Oct	•	6	•							•	14
12	Idlewilde	5,000	Mar-Oct		10	•			•				•	14
13	Pinery Canyon	7,000	Apr-Nov	•	4				•					14
14	Rustler Park	8,500	Apr-Nov	•	22	•			•				•	14

1 Cochise Stronghold

Location: About 57 miles northwest of Douglas, in the Dragoon Mountains.
Sites: 18 tent and RV up to 28 feet. No hookups.
Road conditions: Paved, dirt.
Management: Coronado National Forest, 520-364-3468.
Finding the campground: From Douglas, drive west 2 miles on Arizona Highway 80, then turn right on U.S. Highway 191. Continue 46 miles to Sunsites, then turn left on Ironwood Road, which becomes Forest Road 84. Go 9 miles to the road's end.

Description: This surprising spot, tucked away in a side canyon of the Dragoon Mountains, is dramatically set in Stronghold Canyon East amid shady oaks. There is a nature trail, and a hiking trail leads over Stronghold Pass to Stronghold Canyon West. For many years, this area was the hideout of the famous Chiricahua Apache chief, Cochise, and his loyal followers. Though the campground is open all year, winters can be chilly. Limited services are in Sunsites. The nearest full services are in Willcox and Douglas.

2 Bonita

Location: About 37 miles southeast of Willcox, in the Chiricahua Mountains.
Sites: 26 tent and RV up to 28 feet. No hookups.
Road conditions: Paved.
Management: Chiricahua National Monument, 520-824-3560.
Finding the campground: From Willcox, drive 31 miles southeast on Arizona Highway 186, then turn left onto AZ 181, and continue into Chiricahua National Monument. Go 6 miles to the monument headquarters and the campground.

Description: This pleasant campground, set in pinyon pines, junipers, and oaks on the bottom of Bonita Canyon, is a great base for exploration of the monument. A scenic drive and miles of hiking trails wind through the famous stone hoodoos. The nearest full services are in Willcox.

3 West Turkey Creek

Location: About 49 miles southeast of Willcox, in the Chiricahua Mountains.
Sites: 4 tent and RV up to 16 feet. No hookups.
Road conditions: Paved, dirt.
Management: Coronado National Forest, 520-364-3468.
Finding the campground: From Willcox, drive 31 miles southeast on Arizona Highway 186, then go straight on AZ 181. Continue 10 miles, then turn left onto West Turkey Creek Road, which becomes Forest Road 41. Go 8 miles to the campground, which is on the left.

Description: This small campground, set in oak, pinyon pine, and juniper-forested West Turkey Creek, is an ideal spot when the better-known campgrounds are full. It is also a good base for hikes into the Chiricahua Wilderness. The nearest full services are in Willcox.

4 Sycamore

Location: About 51 miles southeast of Willcox, in the Chiricahua Mountains.
Sites: 5 tent and RV up to 16 feet. No hookups.
Road conditions: Paved, dirt.
Management: Coronado National Forest, 520-364-3468.
Finding the campground: From Willcox, drive 31 miles southeast on Arizona Highway 186, then go straight on AZ 181. Continue 10 miles, then turn left onto West Turkey Creek Road, which becomes Forest Road 41. Go 10 miles to the campground.

Description: Another small campground on the west side of the Chiricahua Mountains, it is primarily of interest to hikers headed for the nearby Chiricahua Wilderness. The nearest services are in Willcox.

5 Bathtub

Location: About 60 miles north of Douglas, in the Chiricahua Mountains.
Sites: 11 tent.
Road conditions: Paved, dirt.
Management: Coronado National Forest, 520-364-3468.
Finding the campground: From Douglas, drive west 2 miles on Arizona Highway 80, then turn right on U.S. Highway 191. Continue 31 miles, then turn right on Rucker Canyon Road. Continue 22 miles, then turn left on Forest Road 74E. Go 5 miles to the campground.

Description: This is one of several small campgrounds in the Rucker Canyon area. This one is reserved for tents only; no trailers or RVs are allowed. The cool, pine-forested canyon is an out-of-the-way spot, and also is a starting point for hiking trips into the Chiricahua Wilderness. Group camping is available at Camp Rucker Group Site. Limited services are available in Elfrida; the nearest full services are in Douglas.

6 Rucker Forest Camp

Location: About 60 miles north of Douglas, in the Chiricahua Mountains.
Sites: 14 tent and RV up to 16 feet. No hookups.
Road conditions: Paved, dirt.
Management: Coronado National Forest, 520-364-3468.
Finding the campground: From Douglas, drive west 2 miles on Arizona Highway 80, then turn right on U.S. Highway 191. Continue 31 miles, then turn right on Rucker Canyon Road. Continue 22 miles, then turn left on Forest Road 74E. Go 5 miles to the campground.

Distant ridges once roamed by members of the Apache Tribe, in the Chiricahua Mountains.

Description: This is the largest of several small campgrounds in the Rucker Canyon area. Limited services are available in Elfrida; the nearest full services are in Douglas.

7 Rucker Lake

Location: About 60 miles north of Douglas, in the Chiricahua Mountains.
Sites: 8 tent and RV up to 16 feet. No hookups.
Road conditions: Paved, dirt.
Management: Coronado National Forest, 520-364-3468.
Finding the campground: From Douglas, drive west 2 miles on Arizona Highway 80, then turn right on U.S. Highway 191. Continue 31 miles, then turn right on Rucker Canyon Road. Continue 22 miles, then turn left on Forest Road 74E. Go 5 miles to the campground.

Description: This is another of several small campgrounds in the Rucker Canyon area. Limited services are available in Elfrida; the nearest full services are in Douglas.

8 Cypress Park

Location: About 60 miles north of Douglas, in the Chiricahua Mountains.
Sites: 7 tent.
Road conditions: Paved, dirt.
Management: Coronado National Forest, 520-364-3468.
Finding the campground: From Douglas, drive west 2 miles on Arizona Highway 80, then turn right on U.S. Highway 191. Continue 31 miles, then turn right

on Rucker Canyon Road. Continue 22 miles, then turn left on Forest Road 74E. Go 4 miles to the campground.

Description: This is the smallest of several small campgrounds in the Rucker Canyon area. Limited services are available in Elfrida; the nearest full services are in Douglas.

9 Herb Martyr

Location: About 63 miles northeast of Douglas, in the Chiricahua Mountains.
Sites: 5 tent.
Road conditions: Paved.
Management: Coronado National Forest, 520-364-3468.
Finding the campground: From Douglas, drive 49 miles northeast on U.S. Highway 80, then turn left on Portal Road. Continue 10 miles, then turn right to remain on Forest Road 42. After 2 miles, turn left on Forest Road 42A. Go 2 miles to the campground.

Description: One of several small campgrounds in the dramatic Portal area, this campground is set in an oak grove next to Cave Creek. It is open to tent campers only; RVs and trailers are not allowed. The campground is a good base for exploring the area; a number of trails lead into the nearby Chiricahua Wilderness. Limited supplies are available in Portal. The nearest full services are in Douglas.

10 Sunny Flat

Location: About 59 miles northeast of Douglas in the Chiricahua Mountains.
Sites: 11 tent and RV up to 28 feet. No hookups.
Road conditions: Paved.
Management: Coronado National Forest, 520-364-3468.
Finding the campground: From Douglas, drive 49 miles northeast on U.S. Highway 80, then turn left on Portal Road. Continue 10 miles, then turn right to remain on Forest Road 42. Turn right again into the campground.

Description: This is another of the small campgrounds in the dramatic Portal area; this campground is set along a meadow, which has excellent views of the surrounding cliff-bound canyons. Limited supplies are available in Portal. The nearest full services are in Douglas.

11 Stewart

Location: About 58 miles northeast of Douglas, in the Chiricahua Mountains.
Sites: 6 tent and RV up to 16 feet. No hookups.
Road conditions: Paved.
Management: Coronado National Forest, 520-364-3468.

Finding the campground: From Douglas, drive 49 miles northeast on U.S. Highway 80, then turn left on Portal Road. Continue 9 miles to the campground, which is on the left.

Description: This is the smallest of the campgrounds in the dramatic Portal area. Limited supplies are available in Portal. The nearest full services are in Douglas.

12 Idlewilde

Location: About 58 miles northeast of Douglas, in the Chiricahua Mountains.
Sites: 10 tent.
Road conditions: Paved.
Management: Coronado National Forest, 520-364-3468.
Finding the campground: From Douglas, drive 49 miles northeast on U.S. Highway 80, then turn left on Portal Road. Continue 9 miles to the campground, which is on the left.

Description: This is the largest and lowest-elevation campground in the dramatic Portal area. A nature trail is located at the nearby ranger station. Limited supplies are available in Portal. The nearest full services are in Douglas.

13 Pinery Canyon

Location: About 68 miles northeast of Douglas, in the Chiricahua Mountains.
Sites: 4 tent and RV up to 16 feet. No hookups.
Road conditions: Paved, dirt.
Management: Coronado National Forest, 520-364-3468.
Finding the campground: From Douglas, drive 49 miles northeast on U.S. Highway 80, then turn left on Portal Road. Continue 10 miles, then turn right to remain on Forest Road 42. Go 2 miles, then stay right again to remain on FR 42. Continue about 7 miles, over Onion Saddle, to the campground, which is on the right.

Description: This is a small, remote campground on the dirt road between Chiricahua National Monument and Portal. It is a good base for those hiking in the Chiricahua Wilderness from the nearby Rustler Park Trailhead. The nearest full services are in Willcox.

14 Rustler Park

Location: About 70 miles northeast of Douglas, in the Chiricahua Mountains.
Sites: 22 tent and RV up to 22 feet. No hookups.
Road conditions: Paved, dirt.
Management: Coronado National Forest, 520-364-3468.
Finding the campground: From Douglas, drive 49 miles northeast on U.S. Highway 80, then turn left on Portal Road. Continue 10 miles, then turn right to

remain on Forest Road 42. Go 2 miles, then stay right again to remain on FR 42. Continue about 6 miles to Onion Saddle, then turn left on Forest Road 42D, the Rustler Park Road. Go 2 miles to the campground.

Description: This is an out-of-the-way campground high in the Chiricahua Mountains. It is a good base for those hiking in the Chiricahua Wilderness from the nearby Rustler Park Trailhead. The nearest full services are in Willcox.

Campground Index

About the author

Bruce Grubbs is an avid camper, backpacker, hiker, mountain biker and cross-country skier who has been exploring the American desert for over 30 years. An outdoor writer and photographer, he has written nine previous FalconGuides. He lives in Flagstaff, Arizona.

FALCON GUIDES ® Leading the Way™

FALCON GUIDES ® are available for where-to-go hiking, mountain biking, rock climbing, walking, scenic driving, fishing, rockhounding, paddling, birding, wildlife viewing, and camping. We also have FalconGuides on essential outdoor skills and subjects and field identification. The following titles are currently available, but this list grows every year. For a free catalog with a complete list of titles, call FALCON toll-free at 1-800-582-2665.

HIKING GUIDES

Hiking Alaska
Hiking Arizona
Hiking Arizona's Cactus Country
Hiking the Beartooths
Hiking Big Bend National Park
Hiking the Bob Marshall Country
Hiking California
Hiking California's Desert Parks
Hiking Carlsbad Caverns
   and Guadalupe Mtns. National Parks
Hiking Colorado
Hiking Colorado, Vol.II
Hiking Colorado's Summits
Hiking Colorado's Weminuche Wilderness
Hiking the Columbia River Gorge
Hiking Florida
Hiking Georgia
Hiking Glacier & Waterton Lakes National Parks
Hiking Grand Canyon National Park
Hiking Grand Staircase-Escalante/Glen Canyon
Hiking Grand Teton National Park
Hiking Great Basin National Park
Hiking Hot Springs in the Pacific Northwest
Hiking Idaho
Hiking Maine
Hiking Michigan
Hiking Minnesota
Hiking Montana
Hiking Mount Rainier National Park
Hiking Mount St. Helens
Hiking Nevada
Hiking New Hampshire
Hiking New Mexico

Hiking New York
Hiking North Carolina
Hiking the North Cascades
Hiking Northern Arizona
Hiking Olympic National Park
Hiking Oregon
Hiking Oregon's Eagle Cap Wilderness
Hiking Oregon's Mount Hood/Badger Creek
Hiking Oregon's Three Sisters Country
Hiking Pennsylvania
Hiking Ruins Seldom Seen
Hiking Shenandoah National Park
Hiking the Sierra Nevada
Hiking South Carolina
Hiking South Dakota's Black Hills Country
Hiking Southern New England
Hiking Tennessee
Hiking Texas
Hiking Utah
Hiking Utah's Summits
Hiking Vermont
Hiking Virginia
Hiking Washington
Hiking Wyoming
Hiking Wyoming's Cloud Peak Wilderness
Hiking Wyoming's Wind River Range
Hiking Yellowstone National Park
Hiking Zion & Bryce Canyon National Parks
The Trail Guide to Bob Marshall Country
Wild Country Companion
Wild Montana
Wild Utah
Wild Virginia

■ *To order any of these books, check with your local bookseller or call FALCON ® at **1-800-582-2665**.*
Visit us on the world wide web at:
www.FalconOutdoors.com

FALCON®

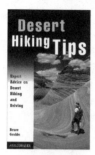
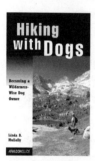

FALCONGUIDES ® Leading the Way™

WILDLIFE VIEWING GUIDES
Alaska Wildlife Viewing Guide
Arizona Wildlife Viewing Guide
California Wildlife Viewing Guide
Colorado Wildlife Viewing Guide
Florida Wildlife Viewing Guide
Indiana Wildlife Vewing Guide
Iowa Wildlife Viewing Guide
Kentucky Wildlife Viewing Guide
Massachusetts Wildlife Viewing Guide
Montana Wildlife Viewing Guide
Nebraska Wildlife Viewing Guide
Nevada Wildlife Viewing Guide
New Hampshire Wildlife Viewing Guide
New Jersey Wildlife Viewing Guide
New Mexico Wildlife Viewing Guide
New York Wildlife Viewing Guide
North Carolina Wildlife Viewing Guide
North Dakota Wildlife Viewing Guide
Ohio Wildlife Viewing Guide
Oregon Wildlife Viewing Guide
Puerto Rico and the Virgin Islands WVG
Tennessee Wildlife Viewing Guide
Texas Wildlife Viewing Guide
Utah Wildlife Viewing Guide
Vermont Wildlife Viewing Guide
Virginia Wildlife Viewing Guide
Washington Wildlife Viewing Guide
West Virginia Wildlife Viewing Guide
Wisconsin Wildlife Viewing Guide

HISTORIC TRAIL GUIDES
Traveling California's Gold Rush Country
Traveling the Lewis & Clark Trail
Traveling the Oregon Trail
Traveler's Guide to the Pony Express Trail

SCENIC DRIVING GUIDES
Scenic Driving Alaska and the Yukon
Scenic Driving Arizona
Scenic Driving the Beartooth Highway
Scenic Driving California
Scenic Driving Colorado
Scenic Driving Florida
Scenic Driving Georgia
Scenic Driving Hawaii
Scenic Driving Idaho
Scenic Driving Indiana
Scenic Driving Kentucky
Scenic Driving Michigan
Scenic Driving Minnesota
Scenic Driving Montana
Scenic Driving New England
Scenic Driving New Mexico
Scenic Driving North Carolina
Scenic Driving Oregon
Scenic Driving the Ozarks including the
    Ouchita Mountains
Scenic Driving Pennsylvania
Scenic Driving Texas
Scenic Driving Utah
Scenic Driving Virginia
Scenic Driving Washington
Scenic Driving Wisconsin
Scenic Driving Wyoming
Scenic Driving Yellowstone & Grand Teton
    National Parks
Back Country Byways
Scenic Byways East & South
Scenic Byways Far West
Scenic Byways Rocky Mountains

■ *To order any of these books, check with your local bookseller*
or call FALCON ® *at **1-800-582-2665**.*
Visit us on the world wide web at:
www.FalconOutdoors.com

FALCON®

FALCON GUIDES ® Leading the Way™

Hiking the National Parks

The national parks have some of the very best hiking in the world, and just because it's in a national park doesn't mean it's crowded. In many parks, the roads are clogged with traffic, but the trails are nearly devoid of people.

As part of the **FALCON** GUIDES ® series, Falcon plans to publish a complete set of hiking guides to every national park with a substantial trail system. If your favorite park isn't on the following list of books currently available, you can plan on it being available soon. Each book comprehensively covers the trails in the parks and includes the necessary trip planning information on access, regulations, weather, etc., to help you put together a memorable adventure.

AVAILABLE NOW:

Hiking Big Bend National Park
Exploring Canyonlands & Arches National Parks
Hiking Carlsbad Caverns & Guadalupe Mountains National Parks
Hiking Glacier & Waterton Lakes National Parks
Hiking Grand Canyon National Park
Hiking Grand Teton National Park
Hiking Great Basin National Park
Hiking Mount Rainier National Park
Hiking Olympic National Park
Hiking Shenandoah National Park
Hiking Yellowstone National Park
Hiking Zion & Bryce Canyon National Parks

ALSO AVAILABLE:
56 state-wide, wilderness-area, and regional hiking guides

TO ORDER:
Check with your local bookseller or
call Falcon at **1-800-582-2665**
www.FalconOutdoors.com

FALCON®

FALCONGUIDES® Leading the Way™

www.FalconOutdoors.com

Since 1979, Falcon has brought you the best in outdoor recreational guidebooks. Now you can access that same reliable and accurate information online.

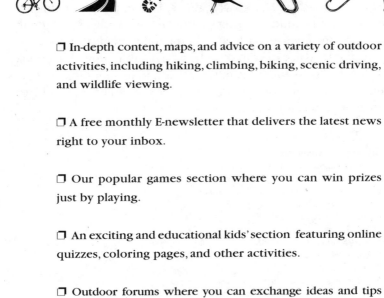

❏ In-depth content, maps, and advice on a variety of outdoor activities, including hiking, climbing, biking, scenic driving, and wildlife viewing.

❏ A free monthly E-newsletter that delivers the latest news right to your inbox.

❏ Our popular games section where you can win prizes just by playing.

❏ An exciting and educational kids' section featuring online quizzes, coloring pages, and other activities.

❏ Outdoor forums where you can exchange ideas and tips with other outdoor enthusiasts.

❏ Also Falcon screensavers, online classified ads, and panoramic photos of spectacular destinations.

Plan your next outdoor adventure at our web site. Point your browser to www.FalconOutdoors.com and get FalconGuided!

FALCON®